Feline Nutrition

Nutrition for the Optimum Health
and Longevity of your Cat

Lynn Curtis

Information is for general information purposes only and is provided without warranty or guarantee of any kind. The content of this book is inspired by the research and observations of professionals. This book is not intended to replace professional advice from your own veterinarian and nothing in this book is intended as a medical diagnosis or treatment. Any questions about your cat's health should be directed to a professional animal health care provider. Please consult your veterinarian before attempting any diet change.

Any company, individual, organization, or product listed in this book, is not an endorsement of such nor does it imply that they endorse this book. Internet addresses and information given in this book were accurate at the time it went to press.

Cover Design by Lynn Curtis
with technical assistance from Jason Chipps

Photographs by Lynn Curtis
with photographic enhancement on the
front cover by Robert Curtis

Copyright © 2011 Lynn Curtis

All rights reserved. No part of this book may be produced or transmitted in any form or by any means without written permission of the author.

Printed in the United States of America.
First Edition: July 2011

ISBN: 1461057337
ISBN-13: 978-1461057338

To order a copy of this book, please visit
www.lynncurtis.com

DEDICATION

This book is dedicated to Ike, my first cat, who succumbed to chronic renal failure at the tender age of nine. Having no nutritional training in my formal education as a veterinary technician, I opted to feed a veterinarian recommended dry diet to him for those nine short years. His loss propelled me on a quest to seek proper nutrition for my future cats.

Through the next decade I continued to learn about feline nutrition, mostly from successes and failures of providing it to my own cats. Now, armed with science and personal experience, I am confident in providing the best nutrition a human can for a cat.

TABLE OF CONTENTS

Acknowledgments	i
Chapter 1 – The Carnivorous Cat	**1**
Obligate Carnivores	1
Chromosomal Evidence	1
Dentition	1
Tongue, Jaws & Musculature	2
Enzymatic Evidence	2
Taurine Requirement	2
Vision & Hearing	2
Vibrissae (Whiskers) & Claws	3
Vitamin Requirements	3
Digestion	3
Taste Receptors	4
Water Chiefly Supplied by Food	4
Fatty Acid Requirements	5
Conclusions	5
Chapter 2 – The Basics	**6**
Intestinal Flora	7
Metabolism	7
Digestibility	8
Bioavailability	8
Chapter 3 – Proteins & Amino Acids	**10**
Essential Amino Acids	11
Naming of Amino Acids	11
Arginine	12
Methionine & Cysteine	12
Threonine	12
Tyrosine	12
Lysine	12
Taurine	13
Carnitine	13
Chapter 4 – Fats & Fatty Acids	**15**
Essential Fatty Acids	15
Arachidonic Acid	16
Eicosapentaenoic Acid	16
Docosahexaenoic Acid	16
Alpha-Linolenic Acid	16

Chapter 5 – Carbohydrates & Fiber	18
Carbohydrates	18
Glucose Conversion	19
Amylase	19
Taste	19
Stomach & Intestinal Contents	20
Fiber	20
Grasses	21
Catnip	21
Chapter 6 – Vitamins	24
Fat Soluble Vitamins	24
Vitamin A	24
Vitamin D	25
Vitamin E	25
Vitamin K	25
Water Soluble Vitamins	25
B Vitamins	26
Vitamin B1	26
Niacin	26
Vitamin B12	26
Biotin	27
Vitamin C	27
Choline	27
Chapter 7 – Minerals	28
Macrominerals & Microminerals	28
Calcium	28
Phosphorus	29
Magnesium	29
Sodium, Potassium & Chloride	31
Iron	31
Copper	31
Iodine	32
Manganese	32
Zinc	32
Selenium	32
Calcium, Phosphorus & Magnesium Ratio	32
Chapter 8 – Water	34

Chapter 9 – Idiopathic Diseases of Cats — 37
Dental Disease — 38
Stomatitis & Feline Oral Resorptive Lesions — 38
Obesity — 39
Hepatic Lipidosis — 41
Pancreatitis — 41
Diabetes — 41
Urinary Tract Problems — 42
Idiopathic Hypercalcemia — 44
Chronic Renal Disease — 45
Hyperthyroidism — 46
Irritable Bowel Disease — 46
Heart Disease — 47
Cancer — 47
Otitis — 47
Allergic Skin Disorders — 47
Asthma — 48

Chapter 10 – FDA & AAFCO Regulations & Guidelines — 49
Labeling — 50
Propylene Glycol Poisoning — 52
Lifestage Formulas — 52
Lite, Low-Calorie Formulas — 52
Product Names — 53
Caloric Statement — 53
Other Label Claims — 54
Report a Pet Food Complaint — 56

Chapter 11 – Interpreting Pet Food Labels — 58
Guaranteed Analysis — 58
As Fed Values — 58
Dry Matter Basis — 59
Metabolizable Energy — 59
Calculating Nutrient Percentages — 60
Calculate the Percentage of Food Weight — 60
Calculate the Percentage of Dry Matter Weight — 61
Calculate the Percentage of Calories — 61

Chapter 12 – Choosing a Commercial Feline Diet — 63
Contamination of Commercial Cat Food — 64
BHT & BHA — 64

Ethoxyquin	64
Selenium	65
Irradiation	65
Heavy Metals	65
Bisphenol A (BPA)	65
Acidifiers	66
Supplements	66
Vitamin K3	66
Onions & Garlic	67
Carrageenan	67
Genetically Modified Organisms	67
Grains, Soy & Carbohydrates	67
Essential Fatty Acid Sources	67
Non-Specified Source Ingredients	67
Meat vs Meat By-Product	68
Meal	68
Yeast	68
Vegetables & Fruits	68
Milk	68
Ash	69
Water	69
Protein Sources	69
Dry Food	69
Semi-Moist Food	70
Canned Food	70
Raw Food	70
Treats & Snacks	70
Optimum Diet	71
Commercial Food Criteria	71
Benefits of a Canned Diet vs a Dry Diet	71
Chapter 13 – Feeding, Daily Caloric Intake & Weight Loss	**73**
Feeding Schedule	73
Daily Caloric Intake	74
Weight Loss	74
Veterinarian Support	75
Chapter 14 – Homemade Raw Cat Food	**76**
Protein Sources	77
Tips	78

Chicken Only Recipe	79
Rabbit & Chicken Recipe	80
Explanation of Ingredients	81
Nutrient Analysis	86
Storage	86
Thawing & Feeding	87
Thawing Raw Food in a Pinch	88
Warming & Serving the Raw Diet	88
Safety & Handling of a Raw Diet	89
Treats & Snacks	90
Benefits of a Raw Diet	90
How to Approach Your Veterinarian Concerning a Raw Diet	91
Chapter 15 – Switching Your Cat to a Wet Diet	**92**
Tips for Making the Switch	93
Appendix A – Useful Websites & Information	**95**
Appendix B – Nutritional Calculations	**96**
Appendix C – Raw Cat Food Recipes	**100**
Appendix D – Supplies for Raw Cat Food Recipes	**102**
Appendix E – Cost Analysis	**104**
Index	**107**

ACKNOWLEDGMENTS

I would like to acknowledge Dr. Lisa Pierson and Dr. Elizabeth Hodgkins for their work in educating cat owners on proper feline nutrition and Natascha Wille for her development of a progressive species-appropriate diet for felines which was the genesis for increased nutritional awareness and health.

I would like to thank, my brother, Robert Curtis, for his photographic expertise on the front cover and for proofing this book and Jason Chipps for his technical assistance with the cover, proofing, and for listening to my endless ranting about feline nutrition.

And it goes without saying, I'd like to thank my cats who endured, albeit stubbornly, the switch from dry to canned to raw food and who now zealously assail their meals without pause.

1 - THE CARNIVOROUS CAT

Obligate Carnivores
Cats are obligate (strict or true) carnivores, meaning they require certain nutrients that they cannot synthesize which are only found in meat. The very name carnivore means devourer of flesh. Cats large and small, wild and domestic need to eat meat as their main source of nutrients. Dogs, bears, and raccoons are all facultative (optional) carnivores or omnivores, meaning they can and do eat both meat and plant matter. However, when given a choice, they will always choose meat if it is available.

A cat is solely designed to hunt, kill, eat, and process meat. Through millions of years of evolution, felids have developed unique characteristics of anatomy, physiology, metabolism, and behavior indicative of obligate carnivores.

Chromosomal Evidence
Domestic cats have 38 chromosomes (strands of DNA in a cell's nucleus that carry genes) while dogs have 78. This demonstrates that cats ceased evolving further after reaching their obligatory carnivorous status, genetically. They never evolved to incorporate plant materials into their diets.

Dentition
Another difference between carnivorous carnivores and omnivorous carnivores is the type of teeth present. Cats have 30 teeth while dogs

have 42. Dogs have more molars for grinding and chewing plant matter while in cats, the upper third premolar and lower molar are adapted as carnassial teeth, suited to tearing and cutting through flesh and bone. These carnassial teeth have no flat crowns for grinding. Meat is digested in the stomach, so there is no need to chew it.

Tongue, Jaws & Musculature
The felid tongue is covered with horny papillae, which help to rasp meat from the bones of their prey.

For the most part, the jaws of the cat only move vertically. This prevents them from being able to chew, but makes it easier for their powerful jaw muscles to hold struggling prey. Cats' heads are highly domed with a short muzzle. The skull has wide zygomatic arches (cheekbones) and a large sagittal crest (ridge of bone running lengthwise along the center of the top of the skull) both of which allow for the attachment of strong jaw muscles.

Enzymatic Evidence
Cats, unlike omnivores, do not have the enzyme, amylase, in their saliva which begins the breakdown of carbohydrates in the mouth. This is required since carbohydrate metabolism takes a long time. Cats utilize the enzyme hexokinase for the metabolism of low-glucose loads in their diet. They lack the ability to metabolize high-glucose loads.

Cats only possess hepatic (liver) enzymes to metabolize a high-protein diet and in lieu of this type of continuous high-meat-protein diet, will start to breakdown their own muscles and organs to achieve this.

Taurine Requirement
Cats have a special need for the amino sulfonic acid, taurine, essential for the formation of bile salts which aid in the digestion of fats and absorption of fat soluble vitamins, healthy eyes, and heart function. Cats are unable to manufacture taurine themselves because they do not have enough of the enzymes to synthesize it from the amino acids methionine and cysteine, therefore, it must be in their diet.

Vision & Hearing
Cats' eyes face forward, allowing for binocular vision for hunting and they have excellent night vision allowing them to hunt their prey,

predominantly small rodents, in very low light. Cats also have excellent depth perception which allows them to move accurately and consistently based on the location of their prey and it is also the reason they are adept at climbing and jumping.

Cats hear high pitched sounds such as those emanating from small rodents. "The hearing range of the cat extends from 48Hz to 85kHz, giving it one of the broadest hearing ranges among mammals."[1] "Analysis suggests that cats evolved extended high-frequency hearing without sacrifice of low-frequency hearing."[2] For comparison, the human hearing range is approximately 20Hz to 20kHz.

Vibrissae (Whiskers) & Claws
A cat's whiskers aid in hunting by moving forward to feel for prey within reach when either the prey is too close or can't be seen by the cat, in bright light or low light. The whiskers also pick up slight vibrations alerting it to prey activity.

Cats have retractable claws for chasing after, grasping, and holding prey.

Vitamin Requirements
Cats cannot synthesize vitamin D from sunlight due to insufficient 7-dehydrocholesterol in their skin and therefore must receive their vitamin D through dietary means (animal products). Meat, eggs, and fish oil are excellent sources while the only vegan source is mushrooms.

Vitamin A occurs naturally, only in animal tissues. While omnivores and herbivores can convert beta-carotene (an inactive form from plants) to vitamin A, cats cannot convert β-carotene into the usable vitamin A they need and therefore need the preformed version from their diet.

Digestion
"The cat's intestine is shorter in proportion to its body size",[3] suggesting that the cat's diet has extremely digestible meat protein and fat for a fast transit time as opposed to fibrous plant material for a prolonged digestive time.

Feline Nutrition

Table 1: Comparison of small intestinal length to body length in selected species.[4]

Species	Ratio
Cat	4:1
Dog	6:1
Rabbit	10:1
Pig	14:1

Intestinal length, as determined by the ratio of intestine to body length, is clearly shorter in cats than omnivores and herbivores. The ratio for cats is 4:1, meaning that the intestines are four times longer than the length of the cat. By contrast, this ratio is 14:1 for pigs, in other words, the intestines are fourteen times longer than the length of the pig, allowing for digestion of a high carbohydrate load.

The larger stomach surface area and nonfunctioning cecum (beginning of the large intestine) in the cat, also indicate a diet of high-meat protein with higher caloric value by limiting the cat's capability to use poorly digestible starches and fiber by bacterial fermentation in the colon.[5] The small and simple stomach of the cat also indicates a highly digestible, multiple meal behavior.[6]

Taste Receptors
A cat's sense of taste differs from other mammals in one important way – cats have a genetic mutation that makes the sweet receptors on their tongues nonfunctional. When cats in a study were presented with sugar-laced water and plain water, they showed no preference for either. This mutation likely helped cats evolve toward all-meat diets.[7]

Water Chiefly Supplied by Food
Dry food is missing the most important nutrient, water. Many cats can and will live a long life on a dry or dry/canned diet, however, we don't know which cats are genetically able to do so until it's too late, typically being diagnosed with chronic renal (kidney) disease. By the time most cats present with chronic renal disease, they have lost more than 70% of kidney function. This is a terminal condition.

Cats have a low thirst drive due to their desert adaptation and do not ingest enough free water to compensate for the lack of water in their diet, and are therefore, chronically dehydrated.

Fatty Acid Requirements
Cats also require an essential fatty acid, arachidonic acid, found only in meat. Cats cannot convert linoleic acid provided by plant sources into arachidonic acid.

Conclusions
Cats, through desert adaptation, require *water* as a component of their food. They also lack the metabolic pathways to efficiently process plant material, thus defining them as *obligate carnivores*; their food should consist only of meat, fat, bones, and organs. These are two very simple yet fundamental facts of feline nutrition.

Many feline diseases such as diabetes, obesity, urinary tract disorders, chronic renal disease, and irritable bowel syndrome can be directly attributed to low moisture, low-meat-protein, and high-carbohydrate levels that plague many of today's commercially produced cat foods.

Many cats *survive* on these dry, supplemented, plant-based diets but they do not *thrive*.

The following chapters will delve deeper into feline physiology explaining how a cat's body metabolizes nutrients. With a basic understanding, optimum choices of either commercial or home-prepared foods may be chosen by the consumer to feed one's cat.

2 – THE BASICS

According to Merriam-Webster dictionary, "nutrition is the act or process of nourishing or being nourished; specifically the sum of the processes by which an animal or plant takes in and *utilizes* food substances."[8] The key word here is utilizes. Although cats, dogs, and even humans can eat many products, it is how we are able to utilize that product or its constituents that makes it nutritious or not.

Many common health problems can be prevented or alleviated with a healthy diet. Conversely, a poor diet can have a deleterious impact on health. The study of nutrition addresses the metabolic and physiologic responses of the body to diet and is concerned with metabolism and metabolic pathways; the sequences of biochemical steps through which substances change from one form to another.

Carnivore and herbivore diets are opposite with basic nitrogen and carbon proportions at varying levels. Carnivores consume high nitrogen and lower carbon diets while herbivores consume lower nitrogen and higher carbon diets.

Much of the current nutritional recommendations for cats and dogs exists as mere minimums and maximums with no optimum level defined. Why is this? Scientists do not know what the optimum levels are. As research continues, the veterinarian and consumer must use their best judgments as to what constitutes an optimally nutritious diet.

For more information on how these minimum and maximum levels are determined, see Chapter 10.

There are six classes of nutrients: protein, fats, carbohydrates, vitamins, minerals, and water which will be discussed in detail in the following chapters.

Intestinal Flora

Animal intestines (including humans) contain a large population of gut flora (microorganisms). They are essential to digestion and are also affected by the food a cat eats and any medications the cat takes. Bacteria in the gut perform many important functions including breaking down and aiding in the absorption of otherwise indigestible food, stimulating cell growth, repressing the growth of harmful bacteria and yeast, training the immune system to respond only to pathogens, production of vitamin C and some B vitamins, and defending against certain infectious diseases.

Metabolism

Metabolism refers to all of the chemical reactions that occur in the living body. This ranges from breaking down calorie containing components such as proteins, carbohydrates, and fats to provide energy, to converting the various nutrients in foods into the protein needed for making muscles, hair and a variety of other structures. An animal gets energy when it ingests food and breaks it down into simpler compounds, which provide fuel to the cells in the body and thus the energy to thrive.

Metabolism is usually divided into two categories. Catabolism breaks down organic matter, for example to harvest energy in cellular respiration and anabolism uses energy to construct components of cells such as proteins.

The chemical reactions of metabolism are organized into metabolic pathways, in which one chemical is transformed through a series of steps into another chemical, by a sequence of enzymes. Enzymes are crucial to metabolism because they allow organisms to drive desirable reactions that require energy which otherwise would not occur by themselves. As enzymes act as catalysts they allow these reactions to proceed quickly and efficiently. Enzymes also allow the regulation of metabolic pathways in response to changes in the cell's environment or signals from other cells.

The metabolism of an organism determines which substances it will find nutritious and which it will find poisonous.

Digestibility

Digestibility refers to the extent to which an eaten nutrient is absorbed from the animal's digestive tract and transported by the blood to the millions of cells in the body. The best way to determine the digestibility of a food is to measure the amount eaten and compare it to the amount passed from the body as stool.

Cats fed extremely cheap food made with low-quality grains and grain by-products will pass more stools per day. The actual volume of these stools might even be more than the amount of food eaten. This is because as indigestible food travels through the animal, it absorbs water which increases its bulk. The digestibility may only be about 70-85% in lower quality foods.

If an animal eats a food that is highly concentrated, more than 90% digestible, it will still produce a stool but perhaps only once a day or every other day. The stool will be well formed and firm.

The digestibility of the food is an important consideration for cat owners. You are paying for the quantity in the bag or can, not the amount your cat digests and absorbs. So, by purchasing a food that has only 80% digestibility as compared to a food that has 95% digestibility, you are paying more of that money for what ends up in the litter box as opposed to your cat. In addition, lower digestibility means more food is required to meet your cat's nutritional needs. Choosing a food simply because it appears inexpensive does not mean that it is truly a good buy. Cost per feeding based on digestibility (and bioavailability) is the only way to determine the actual cost of the food. See Appendix E for a cost analysis.

Bioavailability

Bioavailability of the nutrients present in the food is another concern for cat owners. Many plant materials are not digestible by cats and their nutrients are not bioavailable, meaning, the cat cannot access the nutrient or convert it to a product it needs.

Enzymes play key roles in nutrient synthesis. They are proteins that increase the rate of chemical reactions in cells. Specific enzymes target specific molecules and specific sets of enzymes in a cell determine specific metabolic pathways (series of chemical reactions). When the body is missing an enzyme, the particular chemical reaction associated with it cannot occur. Cats lack certain enzymes for certain chemical reactions. Therefore, they cannot metabolize or breakdown certain molecules, many of which are found in plant matter. Cats require complete amino acid profiles. The result: cats are classified as obligate carnivores.

3 - PROTEINS AND AMINO ACIDS

Proteins are a large group of nitrogen-bearing organic compounds that are essential constituents of living cells. They consist of polymers (chains) of amino acids, the building blocks of tissue, and necessary for the proper formation of hormones, antibodies, skin, hair, muscles and cells that make up many other organ systems. In addition, amino acids are used to make enzymes, which along with vitamins and minerals, are necessary for proper metabolism. Generally speaking, animal-based proteins have a complete amino acid profile; composed of all amino acids. When a cat consumes a diet containing animal protein, the protein is broken into its amino acids and these are absorbed in the small intestine. The amino acids are then reassembled into a different order, making the specific proteins the body needs. Extra amino acids are broken down and used for energy and/or expelled from the body.

In most animals, including dogs and humans, liver enzymes adapt to the amount of protein consumed. This allows the animal to conserve nitrogen (a component of protein) when fed a low-protein diet and excrete nitrogen when fed a high-protein diet. However, cats do not have the ability to regulate protein metabolism. Their bodies are designed to only process high-protein diets. If cats are fed a low-protein diet, their bodies have no choice but to begin converting their own muscle mass to provide energy, resulting in fast weight loss and death. This is significant when considering that many animals, including dogs and humans, are omnivores and eat a wide variety of foods, some of which are high protein and others that are not. In contrast, cats are obligate carnivores and must always consume a high-protein diet. Thus, the protein requirements of cats are much higher than that for dogs or humans.

Of the required amino acids, cats are able to synthesize alanine, asparagine, aspartic acid, cysteine, glutamic acid, glutamine, glycine, proline, selenocysteine, serine, tyrosine, and ornithine (non-essential amino acids) and are unable to synthesize 10 of these (essential amino acids). These 10 amino acids need to be supplemented by the diet.

Essential alpha-amino acids (α-amino acids)

- Arginine
- Histidine
- Isoleucine
- Leucine
- Lysine
- Methionine
- Phenylalanine
- Threonine
- Tryptophan
- Valine

Essential Amino Sulfonic Acid

- Taurine

Conditionally Essential

- Carnitine

When one or more of these amino acids are missing from the diet, food intake typically decreases and weight loss occurs.

Naming of Amino Acids

You may see amino acids listed as L-arginine. The prefix denotes the direction light is rotated and polarized when an amino acid is put into a solution. The Greek root *levo,* refers to left, therefore in L-cysteine, the light is rotated and polarized to the left. The L forms of amino acids are the naturally occurring forms.

The Greek root *dextro,* refers to right, where the light is rotated and polarized to the right such as in D-carnitine. Most of the commercial D forms of amino acids are synthetic, but not all. The body is also able to change the D form to the L form and vice versa. These DL forms (DL-methionine) are optically inactive (racemic).

Only the L forms of amino acids are biosynthesized and incorporated into proteins.

Taurine (an amino sulfonic acid) and glycine (an α-amino acid) do not polarize and rotate light either to the left or to the right so the proper names for them are just taurine and glycine, not L-taurine and L-glycine, however, you will commonly see them listed as such. These two "amino acids" are always in the natural form.

Arginine
Ornithine is used by cats to process urea. Ornithine production in other animals may occur in several different ways, however, the only way for cats to synthesize this amino acid is through its conversion from arginine. They require large amounts of arginine in order to bind ammonia (nitrogen source) produced from the breakdown of protein. Without it, high levels of ammonia accumulate in their blood. Hyperammonemia can occur in cats that are either not eating or have hepatic lipidosis, therefore, arginine supplements may be needed for cats with either or both conditions. It is found in large quantities in meat and eggs.

Methionine & Cysteine
These amino acids are converted to glucose and then used to provide energy. Cysteine is also important for hair growth and for production of felinine, which is excreted in urine and used for scent marking predominantly by intact male cats.

Threonine
The amino acid, threonine, helps prevent fat buildup in the liver. It may be helpful in the treatment of hepatic lipidosis. It is found in large quantities in poultry and meat.

Tyrosine
Many cats manufacture enough tyrosine, however, some will need to acquire it from their diet. Tyrosine is important in the production of melanin. A deficiency in black cats is seen when their hair takes on a reddish brown tinge. (Note: black hair also oxidizes with sunlight to a brownish tinge.)

Lysine
The amino acid, L-lysine is useful as a treatment for the feline herpes virus that produces flu-like symptoms. The herpes virus uses the amino acid arginine to replicate itself. The natural chemical process of arginine

use is limited by the amount of lysine available. Supplementing lysine allows the arginine to be used up by this natural chemical process thereby starving the virus cells and inhibiting growth. Chicken and eggs are excellent sources of lysine.

Taurine (amino sulfonic acid)
Cats have a special need for the amino sulfonic acid, taurine (taurine is not actually an amino acid), essential for the formation of bile salts which aid in the digestion of fats and absorption of fat soluble vitamins, healthy eyes, and heart function. Cats are unable to manufacture taurine themselves because they do not have enough of the enzymes to synthesize it from methionine and cysteine, and so it must be in their diets. Dogs and most other animals can usually make taurine. Only animal-based products contain taurine.

While it has been known since the 1960's that cats required taurine, it was not until the late 1980's that pet food manufacturers realized the effect that processing had on the availability of taurine. One of the leading causes of death in cats at the time (dilated cardiomyopathy, weakening of the heart muscle) could have been prevented by increasing the amount of taurine in the diet. "Cats with advanced stages of cardiomyopathy could be completely cured in as little as 2 to 4 weeks when given a taurine supplement. Since the late 1980's when cat foods were supplemented with additional taurine, the incidence of dilated cardiomyopathy in cats has declined dramatically."[9]

Other signs of taurine deficiency in cats includes blindness (which cannot be reversed with supplemental taurine), reduced fertility in female cats, and abnormal developments in kittens.

Taurine deficiency may take a few months to a few years to present with clinical signs. The pet food companies, in answer to the lack of taurine in their plant-based diets, responded not by adding meat (the only natural source of taurine) thereby replacing most or all of the plant matter, but by supplementing the diet with taurine itself.

Carnitine
Carnitine is thought to be conditionally essential in cats. It is synthesized in the cat's kidneys and is utilized in the cat's body for

metabolizing fatty acids. It is also important in heart health, weight loss, and possibly in the treatment of hepatic lipidosis.

4 - FATS & FATTY ACIDS

Like protein, fats serve as an important energy source for cats. Compared to carbohydrates and proteins, fat is a much more concentrated form of dietary energy, providing more than twice the calories and energy. Fats are more digestible for cats than carbohydrates and supply the essential fatty acid arachidonic acid (required by cats). Fats aid in the absorption of the fat soluble vitamins A, D, E, and K and help make the food more palatable. According to the NRC (National Research Council), cats can tolerate high levels of dietary fats.[10]

Essential Fatty Acids
Essential fatty acids (EFAs) are constituents of triglycerides (esters derived from 3 EFAs plus glycerol) and are required not only for energy but also for biological processes. These acids must be supplied by the diet since they cannot be synthesized.

Cats are unable to convert omega-EFAs from plant sources such as flaxseed oil which has become a popular addition in commercial cat foods. Flaxseed is a great source of EFAs for humans but cats cannot utilize it. Flaxseed oil, as well as soybean, canola, and other vegetable-based oils, contain the fatty acid alpha-linolenic acid which the cat cannot convert to the biologically active forms of eicosapentaenoic acid (EPA) and docosahexaenoic acid (DHA) because they lack the sufficient enzyme activity to do so.

Feline Nutrition

These omega-EFAs (ω-EFAs) are designated according to where the double carbon bond exists from the terminal end of the fatty acid carbon chain. In omega-3 EFAs it is located at the n-3 (ω-3 or omega-3) position, indicating the third to last double bond.

Omega EFAs assist in clotting, are vasodilators, help lower arterial blood pressure, produce healthy skin, reduce arthritis effects, maintain a strong immune system, and inhibit excess production of cholesterol.

A deficiency of essential fatty acids can impair wound healing, cause a dry, lusterless coat and scaly skin, and change the lipid (fat) composition on the skin and coat.

Arachidonic Acid (AA) – Omega-6 EFA
Cats cannot convert linoleic acid to arachidonic acid which is an essential fatty acid for the cat and only found in animal fats. Arachidonic acid is necessary to produce an inflammatory response. In many cases, such as in allergies, the goal is to suppress the inflammatory response. But in other cases, the response is a necessary means by which the body can protect itself.

AA is abundant in the brain, muscles, and liver of animals and is required for growth and repair of skeletal muscle, growth and repair of neurons, and neurological development.

Eicosapentaenoic Acid (EPA) – Omega-3 EFA
Eicosapentaenoic acid is a precursor (substance which forms another) of docosahexaenoic acid. EPA works in conjunction with arachidonic acid. If there is not enough EPA, the inflammatory effects of arachidonic acid will overtake the system and may cause inflammatory-related diseases.

Docosahexaenoic Acid (DHA) – Omega-3 EFA
Docosahexaenoic acid is present in the brain and retina. It is synthesized from EPA and also found abundantly in cold-water oceanic fish which derive it from consuming algae.

Alpha-Linolenic Acid (ALA) – Omega-3 EFA
Alpha-linolenic acid may also be required by the cat. Not much is understood about this fatty acid. However, it can be converted to both

EPA and DHA. Even so, large quantities of ALA are required for this synthesis and the process may be inefficient.

5 – CARBOHYDRATES & FIBER

Carbohydrates
Interestingly, the National Research Council and AAFCO do not give a minimum or maximum amount of carbohydrates in their nutrient profile for cats, yet most commercial cat foods contain high levels of carbohydrates. So far, there is no scientific evidence that cats require any carbohydrates at all.

Carbohydrates come from plant sources such as cereal grains, fruits, and vegetables. Grains are cheap and dry food is convenient. In the United States, corn is cheap and readily available. It also supplies a sizable quantity of protein, however, the cat cannot utilize this type of protein due to reduced bioavailability and low digestibility. Many grasses, including corn, are a rich source of vitamins, minerals, carbohydrates, fats, oils, and protein and although a staple for many human cultures, for cats these products are mostly carbohydrate with the remaining nutrients essentially unavailable.

Carbohydrates are not a required nutrient for obligate carnivores and the body needs of the cat for glucose (energy source for the brain) can easily be met by breaking down triglycerides (the glycerol component can be converted into glucose) and certain (glucogenic) amino acids that can also be converted to glucose, such as methionine and cysteine. When ingesting a high carbohydrate diet, the cat's pancreas responds by releasing more insulin which may cause low blood sugar, which in turns causes the cat to feel hungry, requiring more food. Unfortunately, this cycle causes the accumulation of fat in the cat's body which leads to obesity, all the while, never meeting the protein requirement and potentially setting the cat up for diabetes in the future.

Glucose Conversion

Required hepatic (liver) enzymes for glucose conversion are hexokinase which converts low quantity glucose to energy, which the cat possesses and glucokinase which converts high quantity glucose to energy, which offers only low activity in the cat. Fructokinase is the enzyme responsible for converting both sucrose and fructose; this enzyme is completely absent in the cat.

In simple terms, cats cannot convert sucrose, fructose, or high-quantity glucose. These sugars are not required in the feline diet and if included will be deposited as fat and stored in the cat's body, fostering a possibility for diabetes, obesity, and/or hepatic lipidosis.

Amylase

Salivary amylase is absent from the cat while pancreatic amylase activity is reduced. Amylases are enzymes that break down starches and sugars for conversion into energy.

Taste

A cat's sense of taste differs from other mammals in one important way – cats have a genetic mutation that makes the sweet detectors on their tongues nonfunctional.

"We characterized the sweet-receptor genes of domestic cats as well as those of other members of the Felidae family of obligate carnivores, the tiger and cheetah. Because the mammalian sweet-taste receptor is formed by the dimerization of two proteins (T1R2 and T1R3; gene symbols Tas1r2 and Tas1r3), we identified and sequenced both genes in the cat. The cat Tas1r3 gene is expressed, as expected, in taste buds. Tas1r2 in the tiger and cheetah and in six healthy adult domestic cats all show a similar deletion in the gene. We conclude that cat Tas1r3 is an apparently functional and expressed receptor but that cat Tas1r2 is an unexpressed pseudogene. A functional sweet-taste receptor cannot form, and thus the cat lacks the receptor necessary for detection of sweet stimuli. During the evolution of the cat's strictly carnivorous behavior, selection to maintain a functional receptor was apparently relaxed. This molecular change was very likely an important event in the evolution of the cat's carnivorous behavior."[11]

Additionally, when cats in a study were presented with sugar-laced water and plain water, they showed no preference for either. This mutation helped cats evolve toward all meat diets.[12]

Stomach & Intestinal Contents

As cats do ingest some stomach and intestinal contents of their prey, the carbohydrates are minimal and pre-digested by the prey's own enzymatic juices. When small or large cats eat larger prey, they typically reject both the stomach and intestinal contents by either squeezing out the organs or refusing to eat them at all.

Fiber

Insoluble fibers (cellulose and lignins) move rapidly through the gastrointestinal tract and provide bulk but no calories. For this reason, high-fiber diets are used to reduce the energy content (caloric value) of the diet and have been recommended for overweight animals. In contrast, diets high in fiber are counterintuitive for cats since cats have high meat protein energy requirements and it is not necessary to add to feline diets unless in extremely small amounts. High-fiber diets may also cause constipation in cats.

Although vegetables may provide fiber they also provide carbohydrates. If needed, only small amounts of psyllium husk powder should be added. It has no additives, artificial flavorings, or carbohydrates. Plant material also produces an alkaline environment conducive to bacterial growth and particular types of crystal growth and many plant products produce gas in the digestive system and cause bloating.

Potential problems may also occur when giving a high-fiber diet to felines. Fiber decreases the absorption of taurine and calcium along with other nutrients. Fiber may also attach to other trace minerals prohibiting bioavailability. Chitin or chitin-like fibers in fish such as menhaden may also prohibit bioavailability of certain nutrients. Insoluble fiber will increase fecal volume, inadvertently leading to dehydration.

Bone is actually a good source of fiber in the form of fibrils (very fine fibers).

Grasses

Many cats like to munch on grasses in the wild. Most cats prefer grasses over plants. If your indoor cat is munching on houseplants, it is a good idea to purchase cat grass kits or seeds that you can plant. This way your plants are safe, and so is your cat, because many houseplants are toxic to them. Cat grass should never be fertilized since many fertilizers contain harmful chemicals. It is not a good idea to take grass cuttings from your lawn, either, due to possible contamination with both fertilizers and pesticides.

You can buy kits that come complete with container, soil, and seeds, to plant yourself and others where you just have to add water. The most cost effective way, however, is to buy your own organic soil (never take it from your backyard, it may be infected with parasites) and grass seed from a pet shop. Most cats prefer oat, barley, Kentucky bluegrass, or wheat grass over rye grass, but any will do. Make sure the seeds are not treated if you buy them from a nursery. Any grass seed you buy from a pet shop or seed that is specified for cats should be safe.

Allow your cats to graze on it at free will unless you notice they are eating too much. Eating too much grass can cause vomiting and diarrhea. Restrict them access by allowing them a five minute feeding once per day.

Scientists are unsure why some cats eat a small amount of grass per day since they are obligate carnivores. Some suggest that it adds roughage to the diet and some say that it is a natural laxative to help with the passage of hairballs and help with gastric discomfort.

Catnip

Catnip is a non-toxic and non-addictive perennial herb belonging to the mint family (also known as catmint, catrup, and catwort) which includes oregano, sage, and basil. Catnip, *Nepeta cataria,* now grows wild in North America and Canada after being introduced from its native Mediterranean region. The active ingredient in catnip is nepetalactone which induces a psychosexual response in both male and female cats. Nepetalactone is most concentrated within the leaves of the plant.

About 60-75% of all cats possess the genetic trait, a unique receptor for the nepetalactone molecule. This receptor is located in the vomeronasal organ (Jacobson's organ), a structure positioned above the palate and present in many mammals. Smelling the catnip is what causes cats to react to it, ingestion alone has no effect.

Reactive cats may not show a response if they are too young. Kittens will show their first reaction between three to six months of age while senior cats may no longer show a response at all. Some cats do not develop the penchant until several years old. Some cats require a stress-free environment before they will allow themselves to indulge. Most lions, pumas, and leopards also react to catnip.

The enticing odor of catnip oil triggers certain nerves within the cat's brain, causing many to roll and rub or wallow in it, purring loudly. Other cats lick, drool, jump, and run, eating it and showing inebriated behavior for 5-15 minutes. After the initial "high", most cats sleep it off or remain pacified or calm for several hours. About an hour's removal from the catnip is required before the second dose is effective.

Not all catnip plants are created equal, different plants have different amounts of nepetalactone present. Catnip pellets are usually about 50% stronger than leaves. If a large quantity of fresh catnip is consumed there may be some vomiting or diarrhea, although this is rare. In this case, just limit or withhold catnip from your cat.

Catnip is a natural repellent of cockroaches. Many people plant catnip amongst their flowering plants, borders and hedges to keep harmful insects away such as aphids, mites, caterpillars, beetles, and ants. Chris Peterson and Joel Coats of Iowa State University tested nepetalactone, the active ingredient in catnip, and found that it "repelled roaches at doses only 1 percent as high as the widely used repellent called DEET, therefore it is 10 times as effective."[13] Nepetalactone has also been tested on flies which it killed in its rarer more potent form. At this time there are no cockroach repellents on the market. Catnip is also said to repel rats and mice. Freshly picked catnip leaves can be rubbed onto your pet's coat to drive fleas away. This must be repeated often. In 2009, a team led by Mathias Christmann of Dortmund University of Technology, in Germany, used nepetalactone as the starting material to synthesize (+)-englerin A, a promising human kidney cancer drug.

6 - VITAMINS

There are two main groups of vitamins: water soluble and fat soluble. The water soluble vitamins are not stored to any great extent in the body and excesses are excreted, whereas fat soluble vitamins are stored in fatty tissue and liver and therefore excesses are toxic. The vitamins are:

Fat Soluble
vitamin A
vitamin D
vitamin E
vitamin K

Water Soluble
Thiamin (vitamin B1)
Riboflavin (vitamin B2)
Niacin (vitamin B3)
Pantothenic acid (vitamin B5)
Pyridoxine (vitamin B6)
Biotin (vitamin B7)
Folic acid (vitamin B9)
Cobalamin (vitamin B12)
vitamin C (ascorbic acid)
Choline

Fat Soluble Vitamins
The fat soluble vitamins have very specific functions.

Vitamin A
Vitamin A occurs naturally, only in animal tissues. While omnivores and herbivores can convert β-carotene (beta-carotene) from plants to retinol, the active form of vitamin A, cats cannot because they lack the

proper enzyme to do so; they therefore need the preformed version. In commercial cat foods, it is generally added as retinyl palmitate. The primary functions of vitamin A are helping to maintain proper eyesight, helping in maintenance of normal healthy skin and bone, and for tooth metabolism. Liver is an excellent source of vitamin A.

Vitamin D
Vitamin D helps the body utilize calcium and phosphorus and is critical in the formation and maintenance of bones and teeth. Cats cannot synthesize vitamin D from sunlight due to insufficient 7-dehydrocholesterol in their skin and therefore must receive their vitamin D through dietary means (meat, liver, fat, egg yolks).

Vitamin E
Vitamin E (d-alpha-tocopherol*) is a fat soluble antioxidant that stops the oxidation of fat. Sources are liver and animal fat. When adding any type of fat or oil to the diet, vitamin E is required to prevent breakdown (rancidity) of the fat.

While vitamin E is a fat-soluble vitamin, there is more leeway than the other fat-soluble vitamins, which when taken in excess, will cause toxic levels to be attained.

*As stated in Chapter 3 (Proteins & Amino Acids), most amino acids with the prefix D are synthetic, while the D forms of vitamin E are the natural forms and the L forms are the synthetic forms.

Vitamin K
Vitamin K is important for blood clotting. The synthesis of vitamin K by bacteria in the large intestine of cats can contribute at least a portion, in not all, of the daily requirement. Therefore, a dietary supply of this vitamin only becomes significant when bacterial populations in the large intestine are reduced, such as during medical treatment with certain types of antibiotics, or when there is interference with the absorption or use of vitamin K from bacterial sources. Sources are meat, chicken skin, and egg yolk.

Water Soluble Vitamins
Unlike the fat soluble vitamins, most of the water soluble vitamins function as cofactors in various metabolic reactions, which enable the

animal to extract energy from the ingested fats, proteins, and carbohydrates.

B Vitamins

The B vitamins protect against disease and viruses. The signs of a B-vitamin deficiency are vague, but are usually characterized by a loss of appetite and poor skin and coat, which could also mimic other diseases.

Several B vitamins are synthesized by bacteria in the intestines of healthy cats. Intestinal problems such as diarrhea, excessive drinking and urination, and administration of fluids can eliminate this source, as well as antibiotic use. B vitamin complex may be used for cats that are diabetic or have kidney disease as these conditions cause the flushing of the B vitamins out of the cat's body. B complex also helps with appetite and energy levels.

Vitamin supplementation is often necessary during prolonged illnesses involving the intestine or during prolonged antibiotic treatment. Some B vitamin sources are meat, heart, liver, and egg yolk.

Vitamin B1 (Thiamin or Thiamine)

Thiamin converts glucose to energy. It is important for muscle and nerve cell function. A deficiency can arise in cats which are fed large amounts of seafood which contains an enzyme called thiaminase thereby destroying thiamin. Processing may also destroy most of the thiamin in cat food.

Niacin (Vitamin B3)

Although cats possess the enzymes needed for niacin synthesis from the amino acid tryptophan, they cannot manufacture a sufficient amount for their needs and require it in their diets. Both niacin and tryptophan are found in meat and eggs.

Vitamin B12 (Cobalamin)

Vitamin B12 is only found in animal-based products. It is required for brain and nervous system function, for the formation of blood cells, and is important for fatty acid synthesis for energy. Methylcobalamin is widely used for cats with diabetes and kidney disease. Cyanocobalamin is the synthetic version of vitamin B12.

Biotin (Vitamin B7)
Biotin may become unavailable to cats that have been fed raw egg whites because the egg whites contain avidin, a protein that binds to biotin thereby making it unavailable. Egg whites should always be cooked.

Vitamin C
Vitamin C is not considered to be an essential vitamin in the diet of cats. Cats synthesize sufficient vitamin C (ascorbic acid) from glucose in their small intestine, and the cat's natural prey diet is devoid of a pure source of this vitamin.[14] Additional supplementation can be harmful because excessive ascorbic acid is excreted in the urine as oxalates.[15] A high concentration of oxalate in the urine can contribute to the formation of calcium oxalate stones in the urinary tract, including the kidneys.[16]

A controlled study has also shown that large doses of injectable ascorbic acid have no beneficial effects for preventing or reducing the severity of feline respiratory disease. In addition, an overdose on vitamin C can enhance iron absorption and cause a resulting overdose of this mineral.[17] The cat's resistance to disease is much less dependent on vitamin C, as is the case for humans.

Choline
Choline, while not officially a vitamin, is often included with vitamins due to the fact that it shares some of the same traits, although its requirement is 100 to 1000 times that of most vitamins. Choline functions in a variety of metabolic reactions and also plays an important structural role in cell membranes and nerve transmission. It is found in meat and liver.

7 - MINERALS

Although important for a variety of functions, minerals make up only a small part of the body weight. They are inorganic compounds that cannot be synthesized by the body so therefore must be supplied by the diet. Overall, they are responsible for bones, teeth, maintenance of fluid balance in the body, and metabolic reactions. Minerals can be grouped into either of two categories based on the amount required:

- Macrominerals: inorganic nutrients needed in relatively high daily amounts for which the dietary requirements are expressed as parts per hundred (pph).
- Microminerals: inorganic nutrients needed in minute daily amount for which dietary requirements are expresses as parts per million (ppm).

Macromineral (pph)	Micromineral (ppm)
Calcium	Iron
Phosphorus	Copper
Magnesium	Iodine
Sodium	Manganese
Potassium	Zinc
Chloride	Selenium

Calcium
The primary role of calcium is building bones and teeth and almost all of the calcium in a cat's body is used to build these two structures.

Calcium deficiencies are rare now, but were more common fifty or so years ago and were primarily associated with cats fed all meat diets which contained almost no calcium. Since the advent of commercial diets, calcium deficiencies now are usually the result of owners feeding meat-only items to their cats like canned tuna instead of a balanced diet including meat, organs, and bone.

High calcium intakes can cause secondary trace mineral deficiencies, most notably iron, zinc, and copper. This occurs because the calcium competes with these trace minerals for absorption in the intestine. Since calcium is required in the parts per hundred and the trace minerals are required in parts per million, even a small addition of calcium to a balanced diet can lead to a dramatic reduction in trace mineral absorption and a trace mineral deficiency. Typical signs are bone abnormalities, slow growth in young cats, and skin and hair problems. Bones in the diet provide an excellent source of calcium.

Phosphorus

Phosphorus, like calcium, plays a major role in the development and maintenance of bones and teeth but also plays an important role in cell metabolism. The calcium to phosphorus ratio is extremely important, "although calcium to phosphorus ratios (0.7:1 to 2:1) may be fairly wide. Phosphorus in plant sources is usually present as phytate (phosphorus bound to carbohydrates) and only a small portion of this phosphorus is bioavailable to the cat."[18] In contrast, phosphorus from animal sources and mineral supplements are usually completely available. Meat in the diet provides an excellent source of phosphorus.

Magnesium

Magnesium participates in a variety of body functions including bone metabolism. Magnesium in cat food came into the spotlight in the 1980's. Cats had become prone to urinary tract blockage and one of the most common types of uroliths (crystals/stones) found in cats is struvite, which is composed of ammonium, magnesium, and phosphate. It was once thought that the best way to reduce the risk of these uroliths was to feed a cat a low ash/low magnesium diet.

Magnesium is an essential mineral for cats. It is involved in numerous functions of the body like energy production, formation of urea, and muscle relaxation. Magnesium also prevents tooth decay by binding calcium to tooth enamel, aids in bone growth, and is essential for proper function of the muscles, including the heart. It also helps to regulate the acid-alkaline balance in the body. "Magnesium is the most plentiful cation (positively-charged ion) in soft tissue next to potassium and excessive loss leads to tissue breakdown and cell destruction. Magnesium promotes absorption and metabolism of other minerals like calcium, phosphorus, sodium, and potassium, and helps utilize vitamin E as well as B vitamins."[19]

"A deficiency of dietary magnesium severely affects cardiovascular, neuromuscular, and renal (kidney) tissues, and contributes to calcium deposits in the kidneys (kidney stones), in blood vessels, and in the heart. It can also be the cause of gastrointestinal disorders, irritability, irregular heart rhythm, lack of coordination, muscle twitch, tremors, and weakness. The symptoms of long term dietary deficiency of magnesium are very similar to a deficiency in calcium, including muscle cramps, high blood pressure, and malformation of the bones."[20]

"Cats need magnesium as an essential part of their daily diet and a certain amount of it in relation to other minerals. Restricting dietary magnesium intake does not prevent disease, but may cause disease. Magnesium reacts with other minerals when absorbed by the body, and the diet needs to provide a specific ratio of these interactive minerals for optimal utilization: Ca:P:Mg = 1.3:1:0.06."[21]

"The major source of magnesium for the cat is the bones of its prey. Diets prepared using isolated calcium supplements such as calcium citrate, calcium gluconate, or calcium lactate instead of bone or bone meal, need to be supplemented with magnesium."[22]

The absolute level of magnesium in the feline diet by itself does not contribute to the formation of urinary struvite crystals, provided that it is present in the proper ratio to other minerals in the diet and that other dietary factors support the maintenance of an acidic urinary pH. Experiments using supplemental magnesium chloride in the diet of cats have shown that a "high dietary magnesium intake does not result in any signs of FUS if acidic urine is produced. However, if the urine pH is 7.5 or higher, struvite crystals will form even in cats fed a diet low in magnesium. These facts emphasize the role of urinary pH in the development of FUS in the cat (who has been evolutionarily adapted to produce acidic urine) and not total magnesium content."[23]

"Wild-living, prey-eating cats produce urine with a pH between 6.0 and 7.0. The cat evolved as a desert dwelling animal and is capable of concentrating its urine in order to conserve water (when water is not available or when eating a dry food). The waste products in the cat's urine are very concentrated and include magnesium, ammonium, and phosphate ions that may crystallize in neutral and alkaline urine to form struvite crystals. At a urine pH below 6.6, struvite remains soluble, whereas in a urinary pH above 7.1, crystallization may occur spontaneously. Oxidation of sulfur amino acids during the process of catabolism of amino acids to urea, carbon dioxide, sulfate, and water has acid forming properties. This process does not take place when fats or carbohydrates are catabolized. Therefore, the carnivorous cat eating a largely all meat, high-protein diet will naturally produce low pH or acidic urine."[24]

Sodium, Potassium & Chloride

These minerals are grouped together because they are all electrolytes which share common functions. All of these electrolytes play an important role in regulating fluid and acid-base balance in the body. While most young healthy cats excrete excess electrolytes in the urine, in some older cats or those with a pre-existing disease (heart or kidney disease) this process may be compromised. For these cats, sodium intake is important and should be adjusted accordingly. While sodium is a major health concern in human nutrition, much less is known concerning its effects in cats.

Iron

Iron in combination with proteins and copper forms hemoglobin (the molecule in red blood cells that carries oxygen). Iron is needed continuously to provide hemoglobin for newly produced red blood cells. Low levels of iron will lead to the development of anemia. Liver is high in iron.

Copper

Copper is involved in many processes in the body including the development of bone, connective tissue and collagen. It also aids in the absorption of iron, development of hair pigment and acts as a general antioxidant. It is absorbed from the stomach and intestines and stored in the liver, brain, and kidneys. Some vitamins, for example vitamin C, can inhibit the absorption of copper.

Iodine
Iodine is necessary for the proper functioning of the thyroid gland and the production of thyroid hormones, such as thyroxine. Thyroid hormones regulate the rate of metabolism in the body and play an important role in normal growth.

Manganese
Manganese is important for the proper function of many proteins and fertility and growth. This mineral is stored predominantly in the liver and to a lesser extent in the kidneys, pancreas, and bone.

Zinc
Zinc is an essential mineral for cats. Meat and bone are both good sources of zinc. Zinc is important for healthy skin and hair but also binds to some proteins (metalloproteinases) which are involved in many immunological processes and are a vital part of the inflammatory processes (which prevent infection after injury). The absorption of zinc by the cat's body is rather poor and that is why it must be consumed in the daily diet and considered essential. Its bioavailability is higher in meat than in plant matter.

Selenium
Selenium has a variety of functions. It helps make special proteins, called antioxidant enzymes, which play a role in preventing cell damage. It works with vitamin E as an antioxidant and immunostimulator. Because of its strong ability to stimulate the immune system, it is the most effective defense against some viral infections. Meat, liver, and egg yolks are good sources of selenium.

Calcium, Phosphorus, & Magnesium Ratio
One of the most important issues to address when feeding any feline diet is the calcium-phosphorus-magnesium ratio. Meat contains phosphorus and bones contain calcium. Magnesium is found in both. The average ratio is Ca:P:Mg = 1.3:1:0.06.[25]

For Example:
Ca = 0.513%
P = 0.360%
Mg = 0.025%

To figure out the calcium-phosphorus ratio, make sure the minerals have the same units, typically either a percentage or in milligrams (mg).

Divide the calcium by the phosphorus: 0.513/0.360 = 1.43
Calcium-phosphorus ratio is **1.43:1**.

To figure out the calcium-phosphorus-magnesium ratio, make sure the minerals have the same units, typically either a percentage or in milligrams (mg).

Divide the calcium by the phosphorus: 0.513/0.360 = 1.43
Divide the magnesium by the phosphorus: 0.025/0.360 = 0.07

Calcium-phosphorus-magnesium ratio is **1.43:1:0.07**.

8 - WATER

Water is the most critical nutrient since it makes up 60-75% of the total body weight. Most mammals can lose much of their fat, glycogen, and protein stores and still survive. However, losing a much smaller amount of water can cause death.

Water has unique properties which make it critical for the normal functions of a cell. It is an excellent solvent and most proteins and carbohydrates are readily soluble in water. Even fats, when combined with other molecules, are soluble in water. Water enables the body to transport nutrients to each cell and then transport waste products from the cells and out of the body. Another property of water is its ability to absorb large quantities of heat. Heat is generated within a cell as it metabolizes food. Water helps to absorb the excess heat and slowly distribute it throughout the body where it is eventually lost. Without water, these reactions would damage the cell. Cats have two basic sources of water: metabolic and ingested. Metabolic water results from the breakdown of carbohydrates, fats, and proteins. Ingested water is obtained by drinking or eating foods containing water.

Our cats (*Felis catus*) developed as desert animals in Africa, descending from the African wild cat, still living today, *Felis silvestris lybica*. They lived in the savannah with limited access to rivers and only ephemeral (short-lived) streams and watering holes. Their bodies are designed to take moisture from their prey (small mammals, birds, amphibians, and reptiles) and they do it extremely well. Cats, when presented with a limited water supply, can concentrate their urine and retain as much fluid as possible. Cats have a low thirst drive for this reason (there was no need to evolve such a mechanism for animals that received their daily water requirement from their prey) and unless they receive their water from their food, cats are chronically dehydrated.

"Cats adjust their water intake to the dry matter of their food, not its moisture content. Cats consume 1.5-2 mL (milliliters) of water per gram of dry matter. This is a 2:1 ratio of water to dry matter, which is also the ratio present in their prey."[26] That is, cats on a dry diet as opposed to a wet (canned or raw) diet will essentially consume half the amount of water, even though the dry food contains for example 10% water while the canned food contains about 75% water. As you can see, the amount of water needed to be ingested by drinking to provide satisfactory hydration may be 7-9 ounces per day, something most cats never achieve.

Prey items consist of approximately 65-75% water, canned or raw food typically contains 65-85% water, and dry food contains only about 10-12% water. Cats do not make up the deficit, for dry food, at the water bowl. Cats that are switched from a predominantly dry diet to a wet diet will ingest less free water while doubling urine output. Some cats that have been switched to a canned or raw diet do not drink any water at all since their need is satisfied by their diet.

Table 2: Water intake and urine volume in cats fed dry or wet food.

	Wet Food (mL/day)	Dry Food (mL/day)
Water (in food)	246	6
Water (in addition to food)	32	221
Total Water Intake	278	227
Fecal Water	27	44
Urine	166	79

S. Dru Forrester, DVM, MA, DACVIM - "Management of Lower Urinary Tract Disease"[27]

Proper hydration means better overall health for your cat and can help prevent urinary tract problems, upper respiratory infections, irritable bowel disease, kidney disease, and poor grooming, to name a few.

Fresh, clean water should be available at all times for your cat, no matter what diet is being fed. Always change the water frequently. Cats prefer fresh flowing water and using a pet water fountain may help entice cats to drink.

9 – IDIOPATHIC DISEASES OF CATS

Many of today's feline diseases are treated with medications, often unsuccessfully, without ever considering that the diseases may be based in something so fundamental yet mundane as the diet. In the past two decades, cats have actually decreased their longevity from living into their 20's, to now, living to their teens or even younger. Cats, especially indoor cats that are well cared for and protected, should easily live into their 20's as they had in the years prior to the dry cat food revolution.

Feline diabetes is a manmade disease caused by commercially produced dry foods that are inundated with carbohydrates while other idiopathic (unknown cause) conditions may also be directly attributed to those diets for the same reasons.

The following information applies to cats that have conditions with no known causes (idiopathic). In these cases, it is typical to treat the symptoms instead of the disease itself, since the cause is unknown. Other influences such as cancers, airborne allergens, etc. may also be possible causes for renal disease, skin irritation, or urinary problems. However, a high-meat-protein wet diet will still have positive side effects for most cats with such afflictions. Always consult your veterinarian when making any dietary change, particularly with diabetic cats.

Dental Disease

Consumers have been told that dry food for cats was essential for dental health because dry kibble scrapes and cleans the teeth. Yet, there is no scientific data to support this claim. Cats have sharp pointed teeth so that when they bite down on dry food only the tip of the tooth comes into contact with the kibble, breaking it or shattering it into smaller pieces. None of the hard bits actually come into contact, for abrasive purposes, with the surfaces of the cat's teeth.

Dry food, however, leaves a starchy residue in the mouth and on the teeth. This substance sticks to teeth contributing to tooth decay and gum disease. Cats, unlike omnivores, do not have the enzyme, amylase, in their saliva which begins the breakdown of carbohydrates in the mouth. Many of the "tartar control" formulas of dry kibble contain indigestible fiber which puts a strain on the cat's gastrointestinal tract, as well.

Raw chunked meat helps at least somewhat with dental health. Meat scraping across a cat's teeth as they tear at it will help remove most debris. Small cats, such as our domestic cat, do not chew large bones, (such as chicken bones) as proponents of whole prey feeding purport. Small prey such as mice, rats, small birds, insects, snakes, and lizards are eaten whole or with only one or two bites and these prey generally have small bones.

The acidic aspect of meat inhibits the growth of bacteria. Cats also have an enzyme, lysozyme, in their saliva which attacks bacteria as it enters the mouth by digesting the coating on it, thereby killing it.

Stomatitis & Feline Oral Resorptive Lesions (FORLs)

Feline stomatitis is a common painful and life threatening problem in many cats. Cats having stomatitis often have bad breath (halitosis). They also have red and inflamed gums (gingivitis). In time the inflammation spreads from areas adjacent to teeth to areas more distant (back of the throat or the oropharynx). In some areas, the gums enlarge and block off areas of the oropharynx (cavity at the back of the mouth). Eating and swallowing become difficult and painful for many of these cats. The causes may be disease-related such as FIV (feline immunodeficiency virus) or FCV (feline calicivirus – current vaccine protocols include FCV which will not completely prevent the disease but lessen its severity). It may also be diet-related. As stated previously, carbohydrate-laden food produces a starchy coating on the teeth and in the mouth.

Many cats with stomatitis also have tooth resorption (feline oral resorptive lesions or neck lesions). The inflamed gingiva may appear to be growing into a tooth or the tooth may appear to have a hole. These teeth are extremely painful. The main course of treatment for these cats is usually a surgical procedure involving complete dental extraction with wide excision of the inflamed mucogingival tissues.

No one has yet identified the etiology (cause) and pathogenesis (development) of FORLs. The cause may be complex. The incidence of the disease is much higher today than it was several decades ago. The advent of commercial diets, change in food texture, nutrients, synthetic diet acidification to control feline urologic syndrome, and even magnesium restriction are all factors concerning nutrition that could be responsible. Proponents of a high-meat-protein, wet food diet believe that a switch to a canned or raw diet, along with medications, may provide better long term results without such drastic consequences involving surgical extractions.

Obesity
When ingesting a high carbohydrate diet, the cat's pancreas responds by releasing more insulin which may cause low blood sugar, which in turn causes the cat to feel hungry, requiring more food. Also, low meat protein diets, where the cat cannot down regulate hepatic enzymes, will cause the cat to feel hungry, requiring it to eat more food to attain its protein requirement. Unfortunately, this cycle causes the accumulation of fat in the cat's body which leads to obesity as calories consumed, exceeds calories burned. Cats synthesize protein and fats for energy so carbohydrates are turned to fat in the cat. If you recall from Chapter 5, cats have limited ability to convert high loads of glucose into energy and no ability to convert sucrose and fructose.

A cat's body should be slender and flexible with well-defined shoulders, chest, and waist. There should be a light covering of muscle and fat over the ribs, easily felt with the fingers.

- Normal framed adult cats should weigh between 7 – 12 pounds.
- Large framed adult cats should weigh between 12 – 18 pounds.

Most cats in the United States are now considered overweight or obese. When feeding naturally, cats would ingest a much higher meat protein profile. The cat's body is geared for this diet and when the need is sated the hunger switch is turned off. Cats on a high carbohydrate diet, always feel hungry because they are not ingesting enough of the meat protein and fat they require to function optimally. On the high-meat-protein diet, cats often self-limit, that is, the cat's body recognizes that the caloric protein intake has been met and the cat stops eating. Aside from obesity, this constant onslaught of carbohydrates in a protein-starved body often also produces type II diabetes for the same reasons.

Obesity leads to decreased activity, more weight gain, dry and flaky coat, and the inability to self groom which may lead to infections. Arthritis may then develop as well as depression.

The so-called "weight management" or "reduced" or "lite" foods often remove some fat and increase the fiber/carbohydrate content of the food. Cats on these diets are already starved for protein and fat and the high-fiber diets may cause constipation. Sometimes, these diets are so restricted that the cat is nutrient-starved, chronically dehydrated, and incessantly hungry.

Switching cats to a high-meat-protein, moderate-fat, low-carbohydrate grain-free canned or raw diet will immediately produce weight loss in obese or overweight cats, even without an increase in physical activity. As weight loss progresses, the cat will in turn increase its activity level. As stated above, cats will usually self-limit on this natural type of diet. Normal weight cats will maintain their weight but tone their bodies and underweight cats will generally gain weight with increased muscle tone (lean body mass).

Monitoring weight loss is critical (Chapter 13), particularly in overweight or obese cats. If weight loss progresses too quickly, the cat may stop eating and fat will accumulate in the liver (hepatic lipidosis) causing an emergency situation. Cats should never go more than 24 hours without eating.

Hepatic Lipidosis (Fatty Liver Disease)
With fast weight loss or if your cat has stopped eating, it may develop hepatic lipidosis. Some cases have no known cause, however, most are associated with anorexia. When the cat is fasting (not eating) the cat's body releases large amounts of fat that travels to the liver where it settles and clogs it so much that the liver no longer functions normally. The cat, which may have been eating minimally at this point, will want to eat even less or not at all.

Typically, the best method of treatment is the insertion of a feeding tube into your cat's stomach by your veterinarian. You may then syringe feed your cat through this tube several times a day in your home environment for the duration of recovery. This may be necessary for approximately six weeks but has very good results. As your cat receives the desperately needed protein, it will feel better and eventually begin to eat on its own. At this point, your veterinarian will remove the feeding tube. Hepatic lipidosis usually does not recur.

Pancreatitis
Pancreatitis usually has an unknown cause unless there is trauma, tumors, poison, or infections present. Typical treatment for the dog is a low fat/high carbohydrate diet. There is as of yet, no scientific evidence to support this dietary change in the cat. Once again, a high intake of carbohydrates on a weakened pancreas may cause more problems since the pancreas produces and releases the insulin to metabolize carbohydrates. Pancreatitis may also occur from diets high is polyunsaturated fats without the correct amount of antioxidants (vitamin E). This may happen with the intake of high-fish diets.

Diabetes
As stated above, when ingesting a high carbohydrate diet, the cat's pancreas responds by releasing more insulin which may not be sufficient to metabolize the amount of carbohydrates in its system. Hyperglycemia is indicated by high blood glucose, increased thirst and urine production, increased hunger with weight loss over time, vomiting, dehydration, and lethargy. Usually, insulin injections are required daily, however, in many cats, insulin does not seem to control the diabetes very well and the blood glucose fluctuates widely. "Prescription" diets often contain increased amounts of indigestible

fiber which is supposed to prevent absorption of the sugar into the bloodstream. However, this doesn't seem to work. The high-fiber diet often causes constipation with increased stool volume and still a high blood sugar level. Since this type of diet is not typically palatable to cats, pet food companies add flavor enhancers to entice cats to eat it. And as stated previously, the cat on a high-carbohydrate diet is starved for protein, thereby producing worse results.

Obesity is a common problem of diabetes, however, not all obese cats are diabetic and not all diabetic cats are obese. Corn is one of the main ingredients in cat food due to its availability and cheap cost in the United States. However, corn causes high blood glucose levels because it has a high glycemic index (difference by ranking carbohydrates according to their effect on blood glucose levels).

Diabetic cats that are switched to a high-meat-protein, moderate-fat, low-carbohydrate grain-free canned or raw food, will oftentimes no longer need insulin injections. For those that do still need insulin, the doses are much lower than previously required. Please work in conjunction with your veterinarian on any diet change. Diabetic cats often need their insulin dose decreased within a day or two of beginning this type of diet. If their insulin dose is not evaluated, they could become hypoglycemic (low blood glucose) and die. For a treatment protocol for your veterinarian, please see Appendix A.

Urinary Tract Problems/Feline Urologic Syndrome (FUS)

A urinary tract problem, also called cystitis/FUS/FLUTD (feline lower urinary tract disorder), may present symptoms such as straining in the litter box or blood in the urine. This syndrome is very painful and must be managed with pain medications. A cat that is straining, especially if it is not producing any urine, is in critical condition. *Seek out your veterinarian immediately!*

Quite often, these afflicted cats have blood in their urine. This is typically a result of the irritation (and inflammation) of the mucosal membrane in the urinary bladder from uroliths (crystals or stones) that are present.

While it is rare for a cat to actually have a urinary tract infection, it does happen. The only way to diagnose an infection is by performing a culture and sensitivity to first grow the bacteria to identify it and then to test to see which antibiotics would be effective against it. However, more often than not, the condition is idiopathic. In these cases, it is probable that a dry diet and poor quality nutrition are to blame.

Cats evolved as desert dwellers and receive most, if not all, of their water from their prey. This coupled with their low thirst drive causes them to be chronically dehydrated. Feeding dry food with its inherently low water forces the kidneys to concentrate the urine to allow maximum retention of moisture for the proper hydration of the body. This concentrated urine contains minerals such as magnesium, ammonium, and phosphorus, components of struvite crystals. Struvite crystals may then form, leading to urethral blockage and death.

When urinary tract issues became prevalent, pet food companies realized that the urine produced by these dry, carbohydrate heavy foods was alkaline, a result of carbohydrate metabolism. This is the perfect environment for the growth of struvite crystals. To combat this, the pet food industry chose to add acidifiers to the food to decrease the pH of the urine, typically DL-methionine or ammonium chloride. They also thought it prudent to reduce the amount of magnesium with the idea that if it was not available, the crystals would not form. This entire ideology is counterintuitive. As discussed in Chapter 7, magnesium is critical to the cat for forming bones and teeth as well as other metabolic activities.

The following decade, or so, saw a decrease in struvite crystals and an increase in calcium oxalate stones. Calcium oxalate stones grow in an environment that is too acidic. The prevalence of the calcium oxalate stones is also associated with idiopathic hypercalcemia and chronic acidosis. Acidification of the diet causes, at least in some cases, the leaching of calcium from bone which is then deposited in soft tissues. Production of calcium oxalate stones may also be found in both the kidneys and bladder. Unfortunately, calcium oxalate stones require surgery to be removed.

Male cats are prone to urinary tract problems due to the small diameter of their urethras. Cats that are prescribed urinary diets usually have continued recurrences throughout their lives. Wet diets are required for any cat with urinary issues. These cats should never be fed dry food again.

Interestingly, meat protein produces slightly acidic urine (pH 6.5) which is the natural pH of cat urine and also provides the higher magnesium level required by felines.[28]

Idiopathic Hypercalcemia

Acidifying, magnesium-restricted diets are now viewed as the possible cause of idiopathic hypercalcemia (excess total calcium *and* excess ionized calcium). Ironically, this disease has been increasingly diagnosed since the advent of the urinary diets.[29] It usually affects young to middle-aged cats and is often not clinically recognized, as cats with progressed renal disease usually show a high blood calcium level. Kidney failure causes hypercalcemia and hypercalcemia causes kidney failure and it is often unknown which came first. More often, this idiopathic version is diagnosed fortuitously because of pre-surgical or pre-dental blood work since the condition has few symptoms especially in the mild to moderate forms.

DL-methionine is an acidifier commonly used in many dry cat foods and is also found in some canned versions and some cat treats. There are concerns about chronic acidification and its potentially detrimental effects on kidney function and bone development. Dietary potassium content may also be important because chronic metabolic acidosis can cause potassium depletion which can contribute to renal dysfunction. Urinary diets are typically magnesium-restricted diets, as well. Magnesium is important in binding calcium to bone.

"A change to a high-fiber diet has been recommended with the idea that dietary calcium would be less available for intestinal absorption, but this typically does not change serum calcium levels in these cats for any length of time, if at all. A less acidic diet was also suggested and likewise does not seem to help."[30]

There is evidence that a diet of high-meat-protein such as a canned or raw diet may help these cats. Adding some raw or cooked chicken meat will also help raise the protein level of the food without increasing calcium content. Only small amounts (less than 10% of your cat's daily caloric intake) should be fed, as the meat is not properly balanced since it does not include calcium and other nutrients derived from bone and organs.

Chronic Renal Disease (CRD)

Most cats do not present with CRD until over 70% of their kidneys are no longer functioning properly. Signs include increased thirst and urination, loss of appetite, lethargy, weight loss, muscle wasting, dull coat, and vomiting food and/or bile fluid. Acute renal disease may be treated and cured if the cause is found such as poisoning. Chronic renal disease is a terminal illness and younger and younger cats are presenting with it. Where there is no known cause such as tumor or associated illness or disease, nutrition and water intake may play key roles. There is some indication that the acidosis that occurs due to feeding acidifying diets may also be causing kidney failure with or without hypercalcemia in otherwise healthy cats.

As previously stated, cats evolved as desert dwellers and receive their water with their prey. When cats are diagnosed with CRD, many are immediately put on dry or canned "prescription" formulas with lower protein and phosphorus to alleviate the work the kidneys need to do to metabolize protein. However, as seen before, there is no scientific evidence to support this hypothesis. In fact, giving an obligate carnivore a protein-restricted diet will cause more muscle and organ wasting of an already debilitated body. Once again, we have an unnatural diet the cat refuses to eat which leads to more protein starvation in its weakened state. "Restriction of dietary protein has been recommended for cats with renal disease based primarily on the premise that protein waste is seen in a urinalysis. The potential risks of protein restriction in the cat's diet are however, considerably greater than for the dog. The cat is unable to down-regulate hepatic enzyme activity associated with protein metabolism even when dietary intake is low, thus the cat is particularly at risk of protein malnutrition."[31]

Feeding an obligate carnivore what its body metabolically craves makes more sense; a high-meat-protein diet. Reduction of phosphorus may be necessary but can be done by adding phosphate binders to the food. Another method is to add chopped cooked egg white thereby increasing the protein level without increasing the phosphorus level as egg whites have little phosphorus content. One of the liver chemistry tests done to diagnose CRD is the blood urea nitrogen (BUN) test.

Typically when this number is over the reference range, it is a clear sign along with other factors of kidney disease. However, BUN is a non-toxic by-product of protein metabolism. In fact, some cats on a high-meat-protein diet have BUN levels inherently higher than the laboratories' safe range limits.

Along with diet change to a wet high-meat-protein food with or without phosphate binders and cooked egg white, medications are used for control of hypertension and other side effects of the kidney disease as well as palliative (pain control) care for the cat. Subcutaneous fluid therapy may also be indicated and can be done at home by the owner. Vitamin B complex particularly methylcobalamin a type of vitamin B12 may help CRD cats as it improves appetite and energy levels. For additional help with a diet for a CRD cat, please see Appendix A.

Hyperthyroidism
Hyperthyroidism is the body's production of excessive thyroid hormone. If there is no known cause such as neoplasia (tumor growth), diet may be the answer. Increasingly common, soy products in cat food may be a possible cause. Soy in human food causes similar problems in humans. Increased appetite, weight loss, vomiting, diarrhea, increased thirst and urine production, and restlessness may all be symptoms. This disease is common in cats over ten years of age. Many cats with hyperthyroidism also have kidney disease and hypertension (high blood pressure).

A high-meat-protein, moderate-fat, low-carbohydrate wet diet is indicated with phosphate binders and/or chopped cooked egg white along with management of kidney disease. Hyperthyroidism is safely and effectively treated with iodine treatments and/or surgery.

Irritable Bowel Disease (IBD)
IBD is an immune-related disease featuring chronic vomiting, diarrhea, and abnormal digestive functions in the intestines and/or stomach of the cat. Food is the most obvious allergen which causes these problems. As a response, to these gastrointestinal issues, pet food manufacturers produced hypoallergenic diets, usually containing ingredients new to the cat, such as lamb and rice (fish and beef are common allergens to cats). However, the balance of the ingredients including carbohydrates, vegetables, and fruits, etc. can still produce an

adverse reaction. Typically, both the dry and wet varieties of most hypoallergenic cat foods still do not provide relief. In these cases, a raw diet is the only option.

Heart Disease
When heart disease is diagnosed, a high protein diet with additional chopped cooked egg white will increase the protein content without increasing the salt content. Additional medications will be needed to manage the disease.

Cancer
"For many types of cancer, increasing protein and fat and reducing carbohydrates in the diet can help to slow tumor growth and prevent cancer cachexia (weight loss due to the effects of cancer). It is also important to increase omega-3 fatty acids, found in fish oil (such as salmon oil, *not cod liver oil*), and decrease omega-6 fatty acids (inflammatory) particularly found in plant oils."[32] Flaxseed oil should not be used in place of fish oil, as the form of omega-3 fatty acid found in plants must be converted to EPA in order to be utilized by cats and this conversion does not happen in the cat. "Flaxseed oil also contains some omega-6 fatty acids, which should be avoided."[33] Raw diets are particularly helpful for feline cancer patients.

Otitis
Otitis is an inflammation of the ear. It may involve the outer ear – otitis externa, middle ear – otitis media, and/or the inner ear – otitis interna. Although usually not life-threatening, ear infections are often very painful for your cat. In some cats, ear infections tend to recur after treatments. Chronic infections cause the ear canal tissue to become thick and rough. This can severely impair hearing and may lead to deafness. Many cases involve parasites or other known causes but when otitis is possibly caused by an allergen, switching to a canned high-meat-protein hypoallergenic diet or raw diet may help give relief to the symptoms. This is usually coupled with medications to assist with the control of infection.

Allergic Skin Disease
This disease usually presents with itchy, scratchy skin that may also include dry hair coat and flaky skin. Scratching and itching makes the skin raw and can cause lesions. Switching to a canned high-meat-

protein hypoallergenic diet or raw diet along with medications is the protocol.

Asthma

Asthma attacks can be mild or severe. Symptoms include labored breathing, increase respiratory rate, lethargy, gagging, wheezing, shortness of breath, blue lips and gums, and hacking cough. Symptoms may come and go. Some cats only exhibit mild symptoms such as quiet wheezing and soft coughing. Many affected cats are free of symptoms between periods of breathing problems. Asthma may be due to an upper respiratory infection, heartworm infection, lungworms, cancers, or heart problems. If diagnosis of a particular cause belies discovery, then switching to a high-meat-protein hypoallergenic canned or raw diet with associated medications may help.

As you can see, many diseases or conditions may improve or be resolved, even kidney disease and diabetes, respectively, by providing a species-appropriate diet. One that cats evolved naturally to eat.

10 – FDA & AAFCO REGULATIONS AND GUIDELINES

AAFCO (Association of American Feed Control Officials) requires all pet food labels to contain certain information. In the United States, all pet food is regulated by the Food and Drug Administration (FDA), the United States Department of Agriculture (USDA), and the Federal Trade Commission (FTC). It is further regulated at the state level.

AAFCO establishes standards on which states base their feed laws and regulations, but of itself, has no regulatory authority. These standards such as nutrient content are adopted from the National Research Council's (NRC), of the US National Academy of Sciences, recommendations for cats.

The FDA is charged with the enforcement of the Federal Food, Drug and Cosmetic Act. Under the Act, a part of FDA's responsibility is to ensure that human and animal foods are safe and properly labeled. Within FDA, the Center for Veterinary Medicine (CVM) is responsible for the regulation of animal drugs, medicated feeds, food additives, and feed ingredients, including pet foods. The regulations based, in part, on this law are found in the *Code of Federal Regulations*, Title 21, Food and Drugs, Part 500.

There is however, no requirement that pet foods have pre-market approval by the FDA. The FDA does require that pet foods, like human foods, be safe to eat, produced under sanitary conditions, contain no harmful substances, and be truthfully labeled. Additionally, canned pet foods must be processed in conformance with low acid canned food regulations. (Title 21, *Code of Federal Regulations*, Part 113, abbreviated as 21 CFR 113). Under Section 402(b)(2) of the FD&C Act, 21 U.S.C. § 342(b)(2), a food is deemed to be adulterated if any substance has been substituted or omitted wholly or in part therefrom.

According to the FSMA (Food Safety Modernization Act), signed into law in January 2011, the FDA now has the authority to keep suspected adulterated pet food off of the shelves, which previously was only permitted by the State Departments of Agriculture. This rule goes into effect July 2011.

Labeling

Pet food labeling is regulated at two levels. The federal regulations, enforced by the FDA, establish standards applicable for all animal feeds: proper identification of product, net quantity statement, manufacturer's name and address, and proper listing of ingredients. Some states also enforce their own labeling regulations. Many states have adopted the model pet food regulations established by AAFCO. These regulations are more specific in nature, covering aspects of labeling such as the product name, the guaranteed analysis, the nutritional adequacy statement, feeding directions, and caloric statements.

Cat foods labeled as "complete and balanced" must meet standards established by AAFCO in one of three ways. Cat Food Nutrient Profiles were last updated in 2006 by AAFCO's Feline Nutrition Expert Subcommittee. The updated profiles replaced the previous recommendations set by the NRC.

Manufacturers may choose one of the following methods to entitle them to place the "complete and balanced" statement on their pet food product. (Title 21, *Code of Federal Regulations*, Part 113, abbreviated as 21 CFR 113).

Method 1 – Feeding Trial

Products that are substantiated to be complete and balanced by feeding trials will have the statement "animal feeding tests using AAFCO procedures substantiate that (name of product) provides complete and balanced nutrition".

This protocol requires that 6 out of 8 animals complete a 26 week feeding trial without showing clinical or pathological signs of nutritional deficiency or excess. The cats' general health is evaluated by a veterinarian before and after the test. Four blood values, hemoglobin, packed cell volume, serum alkaline phosphatase, and serum albumin are measured after the trial and the average values of the test subjects must meet minimum levels. No animal is allowed to lose more than 15% of its starting weight.

Method 2 – Nutrient Profile
Products that are formulated with ingredients to meet the established nutrient profile would include the following statement. "(Name of product) is formulated to meet the nutritional levels established by AAFCO Cat Food Nutrient Profiles." There are two separate nutrient profiles: one for "growth and reproduction" and one for "adult maintenance". The nutritional adequacy statement would indicate information on which life stages the product is suitable for. A product labeled as "for all life stages" must meet the more stringent nutrient profile for "growth and reproduction". Products labeled as "intended for intermittent or supplemental feeding" do not meet either profile.

Method 3 – Nutritionally Similar
A third method allows a manufacturer to have a product that is "nutritionally similar" to another product in the same "family" to adopt the latter's "complete and balanced" statement without itself undergoing any feeding tests. The modified statement would read "(name of product) provides complete and balanced nutrition for (growth and reproduction/adult maintenance) and is comparable in nutritional adequacy to a product which has been substantiated using AAFCO feeding tests".

A manufacturer can choose to not meet AAFCO standards, but must put a disclaimer on the product that states that the cat food is for occasional snack feeding only.

Propylene Glycol Poisoning

Propylene glycol was used as a moistener in semi-moist pet foods, which helped retain water and gave those products their unique texture and taste. It was affirmed Generally Recognized as Safe (GRAS) for use in human and animal food before the advent of semi-moist foods. It was known for some time that propylene glycol caused Heinz body formation (small clumps of protein) in the red blood cells of cats, but it could not be shown to cause anemia or other clinical effects. However, propylene glycol reduces the red blood cell survival time, renders red blood cells more susceptible to oxidative damage, and has other adverse effects in cats consuming the substance at levels found in semi-moist food. In light of this data, the CVM amended the regulations to expressly prohibit the use of propylene glycol in cat foods.

Lifestage Formulas

Most pet food companies produce lifestage (kitten, junior, adult, senior, and/or geriatric) formulas of their cat foods. If you look closely at the ingredients, you'll notice that most of the formulas contain the same ingredients most often in the same quantities. Currently, there are only two formulas defined by AAFCO, kitten (growth and reproduction) and adult maintenance, so there are obviously no guidelines for what should constitute a senior cat pet food.

AAFCO at this time does not regulate the term "senior" when applied to commercial cat food. They have not set any dietary requirements or limits on any nutrients in the food. When compared side by side, between *competing* brands, senior foods vary widely in their content both in ingredients and nutrition. These foods still only comply with AAFCO's standard nutrition profile (minimums and maximums) for adult cat maintenance.

Lite, Low-Calorie Formulas

AAFCO regulates what low-calorie cat food implies. However, most foods are dry and have increased fiber to make the cat feel full. This only makes the cat hungrier because the high-meat-protein and moderate-fat requirement has not yet been met and most cats will actually gain weight on these diets. This results in the care-giver decreasing the quantity of food, believing the cat is receiving too many calories, further exacerbating the situation by starving the cat.

Product Names (Title 21, *Code of Federal Regulations*, Part 113, abbreviated as 21 CFR 113).

- **95% Rule** – At least 95% of the food must be the named ingredient. For example, "Chicken for Cats" or "Salmon Cat Food" must be 95% chicken or salmon, respectively. If the food is "Chicken and Rice Cat Food", the chicken is the component that must be 95%. If there is a combination of ingredients such as "Chicken and Liver *for* Cats", the two together must make up 95% of the total weight and the first ingredient must be the one in higher percent in the food.

- **25% or Dinner Rule** – When the named product contains at least 25% but less than 95% of the total weight, the name must include a descriptive term such as "dinner". For example, "dinner", "entrée", "grill", "platter", "formula" are all terms that are used to describe this type of product. For example, "Chicken Dinner Cat Food" must contain at least 25% chicken. This food could contain beef and even more beef than chicken. It is important to read the label and check what other meat sources the product contains.

- **3% or With Rule** – Many times the "with" label identifies extra or special ingredients, such as "Beef Dinner for Cats with Salmon" is a food containing at least 25% beef and at least 3% salmon. "Cat Food with Chicken" only contains 3% chicken but "Chicken Cat Food" contains at least 95% chicken.

- **Flavor Rule** – In this situation, a specific percentage of meat is not required, but it must contain an amount of flavor sufficient to be detected. For example, "Chicken Flavor Cat Food" may contain a digest or enough chicken fat to flavor the food, but there may be no actual chicken meat in it.

Calorie Statement

Pet foods can vary greatly in caloric content, even among foods of the same type (dry, canned) and formulated for the same life stage. Feeding directions vary among manufacturers, too, so the number of calories delivered in a daily meal of one food may be quite different from another. The best way for consumers to compare products and determine how much to feed is to know the caloric content. AAFCO regulations have been developed to allow manufacturers to substantiate calorie content and include a voluntary statement.

If a calorie statement is made on the label, it must be expressed on a "kilocalories per kilogram" basis. Kilocalories are the same as the Calories consumers are used to seeing on food labels. That is, 1kcal=1 Cal. A kilogram is a unit of metric measurement equal to 2.2 pounds. Manufacturers are also allowed to express the calories in familiar household units for example, per cup, or per can along with the required kilocalories per kilogram statement. Even without this additional information, however, consumers can make meaningful comparisons between products and pick the product best suited for their cats' needs. As with the guaranteed analysis, the calorie statement is made on an "as fed" basis, so corrections for moisture content must be made as described in Chapter 11.

Other Label Claims
Many pet foods are labeled as "premium" and some now are "super premium" and even "ultra premium". Other products are touted as "gourmet" items. Products labeled as such are not required to contain any different or higher quality ingredients, nor are they held up to any higher nutritional standards than are any other adult maintenance or kitten formula.

The term "natural" is often used on pet food labels, although the term does not have an official definition. AAFCO has developed a feed term definition for what types of ingredients can be considered "natural" and "Guidelines for Natural Claims" for pet foods. For the most part, "natural" can be construed as equivalent to a lack of artificial flavors, artificial colors, or artificial preservatives in the product. Artificial colors are not really necessary, except to please the pet owner's eye. If used, they must be from approved sources, the same as for human foods. Especially for high-fat dry products, some form of preservative must be used to prevent rancidity (oxidative damage). Natural-source preservatives, such as mixed tocopherols (a source of vitamin E), can be used in place of artificial preservatives.

"Natural" is not the same as "organic". The latter term refers to the conditions under which the plants were grown or animals were raised. There are no official rules governing the labeling of organic foods for pets at this time, but the USDA is developing regulations dictating what types of synthetic additives, such as vitamins and purified amino acids, may be used in pet foods labeled as organic.

Regulations need to be enforced and modified, however, the Pet Food Institute, which is a trade association representing the manufacturers of most dog and cat food produced in the United States, represents the pet food industry before federal and state governments. With the billions of dollars backing this group, it is difficult, to say the least, to alter the regulations dealing with pet food or to establish new ones.

In addition, AAFCO's minimums and maximums are not necessarily valid. There is no specific scientific data to support many of the values as they pertain to total nutrition and metabolic activity as most of the values reached came from limiting or maximizing one ingredient at a time in feeding trials. The table below shows some nutrient information for a rat carcass as compared to AAFCO's minimums and maximums for adult maintenance cat food. As you can see, there are huge discrepancies in many of them. Also, some ranges are actually useless because they are too broad (vitamin A for example).

Table 3: Comparison of nutrient profiles between a rat carcass[34] and AAFCO's[35] nutrient allowances for adult feline maintenance.

Nutrient DMB	Rat Carcass	AAFCO Min	AAFCO Max
Protein	55%	26%	
Fat	38.1%	9%	
Calcium	1.15%	0.60%	
Phosphorus	0.98%	0.50%	
Magnesium	0.08%	0.04%	
Linoleic Acid	9.1%	0.50%	
Iron	288 mg/kg	80 mg/kg	
Vitamin A	84,800 IU/kg	5,000 IU/kg	750,000 IU/kg
Niacin	156.6 mg/kg	60 mg/kg	

Ideally, the following objectives should be met by AAFCO and the FDA/CVM:

- Optimum nutritional requirements for long life, high quality of life, and to minimize disease (thrive vs survive) based on bioavailability and digestibility.
- Requiring pet food labels to include carbohydrate content.
- Requiring pet food labels to list nutritional information on dry matter basis only (see Chapter 11).
- Analyzing possible adulterated ingredients such as ethoxyquin, inorganic selenium, menadione, and other questionable ingredients.
- Allowing ingredient grading such as USDA inspected and organic.
- Inclusion on label of additives that are put in prior to manufacturing facility.
- Better regulations for ingredients generally recognized as safe (GRAS).
- Change protocols for foods to be accepted as "complete and balanced".
- Requiring source of ingredients to be listed on company's website.
- Analyzing and possible denial of use of rendered ingredients.
- Updating and simplifying ingredient definitions.
- Standardize trace heavy metal levels allowable in pet food.
- Removal of food from veterinary offices, as this implies a conflict of interest.

Critics of the AAFCO standards argue that such requirements are too lax. Although maximum levels of intake of some nutrients have been established because of concerns with overnutrition, many still lack maximum allowed levels and some contain a large disparity between the maximum and minimum values. The NRC accepts that despite ongoing research, large gaps still exist in the knowledge of quantitative nutritional information for specific nutrients. With such broad guidelines and loose feeding trial standards, critics argue the term "complete and balanced" to be inaccurate and even deceptive.

Report a Pet Food Complaint
You may now report a pet food complaint directly to the FDA through its Safety Reporting Portal (see Appendix A). Make sure you provide all

of the requested information for them to better handle a recall and for further legal actions. Keep the food product in a sealed container so they have a sample to test or they will not be able to follow-up on the complaint.

Also, file a complaint with your State Department of Agriculture who will in turn communicate with the FDA who now has the power to pull the pet food off of the shelves. Beginning in July 2011, the FDA will be able to force recalls from pet food companies.

Have your veterinarian file a complaint with the FDA, as well.

11 – INTERPRETING PET FOOD LABELS

As stated in the previous chapter, AAFCO requires all pet food labels to contain certain information. Unfortunately, on pet food labels, the information is both incomplete and confusing.

Guaranteed Analysis (GA)
Guaranteed Analysis values are simply a range (minimums and maximums) of the levels of water, protein, fat, etc. that are contained in the cat food. So, if the label states that there is a minimum of 6% fat, there could be 12% fat in the food as long as the quantity is 6% or higher. Ideally, the label should contain the more accurate As Fed (exact measurement) and Dry Matter Basis (removal of water) values or the percentage of calories (metabolizable energy profile).

As Fed Values (AF)
The exact or As Fed values are the actual measurements of the ingredients in a sample of the food. These values more accurately reflect what is in the product (unlike the GA with minimums and maximums). Obviously, between different production runs of food, there will be variations, but these variations will be minimal. Some companies list these As Fed values on their websites, if not, you may request this information from the manufacturers. Like the GA, the AF values also include the water content of the food so it is impossible to directly compare canned food to dry food by comparing the numbers listed on the package label.

Dry Matter Basis (DMB or DM)

Dry Matter Basis removes the water from the equation. When foods are considered on a dry matter basis, they can be directly compared to one another. In other words, a canned food with 78% water can now be compared to a dry food that contains 11% water.

At first glance, it appears that the dry food below has more protein than the canned food. However, the canned food on a dry matter basis contains 45% protein as opposed to the dry food which contains 40% protein, when calculated.

Dry Food		Canned Food	
Protein	36%	Protein	10%
Fat	18%	Fat	5%
Moisture	11%	Moisture	78%

Calculating the DMB (Dry Matter Basis)

Dry Food Protein = 36%
Dry Food Moisture = 11%
100% (dry and wet) − 11% (wet) = 89% dry
(36% Protein / 89% dry) x 100 = **40% Protein DMB in dry food**

Canned Food Protein = 10%
Canned Food Moisture = 78%
100% (dry and wet) − 78% (wet) = 22% dry
(10% Protein / 22% dry) x 100 = **45% Protein DMB in canned food**

Metabolizable Energy (MBE or ME) – Calorie Content

Metabolizable energy (total calorie content) is the most accurate way to compare foods with one another. This measurement disregards any part of the food that does not provide calories such as moisture, ash, or fiber. It only considers the fact that calories are derived from the protein, fat, and carbohydrate portion of the food.

Pet food companies currently list these values on some labels but they can usually be acquired from their website and may appear, for example, as 1,411 kcal/kg.

Feline Nutrition

However, an even better assessment would be the ME Profile (metabolizable energy profile) which would list calories from protein, fat, and carbohydrates individually for comparison.

Calculating Nutrient Percentages

Unfortunately, it is rare to see the carbohydrates listed for cat foods. If companies do offer this information, it is usually only found on their websites. This value, however, is just as important as the protein and fat content. There are three basic methods used to calculate the value of an individual nutrient using either the GA or AF values (always use the AF values when possible, as they are more accurate):

1. As a percentage of food weight (includes water).
2. As a percentage of dry matter weight (no water).
3. As a percentage of calories (no water).

It is best to view the nutrient by the percentage of calories it provides, however, most manufacturers use the weight percentage instead. Although the Guaranteed Analysis values are not accurate (they can be found on the labels of all pet foods), they will give you an estimate of the percentages of the nutrients in the food. It is best to contact the manufacturer for the As Fed values for your calculations. These are sometimes posted on the companies' websites.

1. Calculate the Percentage of Food Weight

To calculate the approximate weight of the carbohydrate in a food, add up the values for protein, fat, moisture, fiber, and ash and subtract this value from 100%.

As Fed Values per 100 grams

Protein	10%
Fat	5%
Moisture	78%
Fiber	1%
Ash	1.95%

10 + 5 + 78 + 1 + 1.95 = 95.95%
100% - 95.95% = **4.05% Carbohydrate Weight**

2. Calculate the Percentage of Dry Matter Weight

Dry Matter Basis removes the water from the equation.
Convert 4.05% Carbohydrate Weight to DMB
100% (dry and wet) - 78% (wet) = 22% dry
(4.05% Carbohydrate / 22% dry) x 100 = **18% Carbohydrate DMB**

3. Calculate the Percentage of Calories

This is the best method for comparing values.
A cat should not receive more than 10% of their daily dietary calories from carbohydrates, less than 5% is best.

Protein and Carbohydrates contribute 4 calories per gram.
Fat contributes 9 calories per gram.

For conversion, you may use either the GA values or the AF values. Whichever method you choose to use for the calculations, make sure to remain consistent with all values. AF values are more accurate.

As Fed Values per 100 grams

Protein	10%
Fat	5%
Moisture	78%
Fiber	1%
Ash	1.95%
Carbohydrates	4.05%

10g Protein x 4 Calories = 40 Calories Protein
5 g Fat x 9 Calories = 45 Calories Fat
4.05 g Carbohydrate x 4 Calories = 16.2 Calories Carbohydrates

40 Cal Protein + 45 Cal Fat + 16.2 Cal Carbohydrates = 101.2 Calories per 100 grams of food ($\approx$3.5 ounces)

To calculate the percentage we must divide the calories for each nutrient by the total calories in 100 grams of food:
(40 Cal of Protein / 101.2 Cal) x 100 = **39.5% Calories from Protein**
(45 Cal of Fat / 101.2 Cal) x 100 = **44.5% Calories from Fat**
(16.2 Cal of Carbohydrates / 101.2 Cal) x 100 = **16% Calories from Carbohydrates**

Using these equations will allow you to compare foods that are processed differently (wet versus dry) and include differing amounts of nutrients (protein, fats, and carbohydrates). Calculating the dry matter basis or caloric content of the ingredients will help you make a better commercial food choice for your cat. Many commercial foods contain between 30-50% DMB carbohydrates. Providing your cat with a diet that is under 10% DMB carbohydrates daily caloric intake is a much better choice.

If at all possible, always acquire the As Fed values from the manufacturer so you may calculate the most accurate results, either converting them to a dry matter basis or calculating the percentage of calories for each nutrient.

12 – CHOOSING A COMMERCIAL FELINE DIET

Choosing a commercial food for your cat may be one of the most important choices you make for your cat in its lifetime. Commercially produced cat foods vary immensely in quality and as you have seen from the previous chapter, reading the labels may be misleading.

In the 1980's, cats were being kept indoors much more often in the United States than previously. Many cats were now indoor only pets. They were protected from disease, fighting, auto accidents, predators, parasites, pesticides, fertilizers, antifreeze, and were more commonly neutered. Pet food companies capitalized on this by producing convenient and economical dry food for cats. In order to formulize cat food, companies took their dry dog food recipes and slightly altered them making the food more cat-appropriate. However, they found that cats would not eat this carbohydrate laden formula so they devised a method of spraying animal digest (fermented entrails) onto the food to make it more palatable for the carnivorous cat. It worked. We now have carbohydrate addicted carnivores (carbohydrate junkies).

Most kitten food is actually healthier and more nutritionally complete for adults than adult maintenance cat food. Kitten foods contain higher quantities of meat protein and fat for growing kittens and pregnant or lactating queens. These formulas much more closely resemble a species-appropriate diet for the feline, as long as they are consumed in the wet form.

Below you will learn what ingredients to choose and which to avoid when comparing and selecting a commercial cat food.

Contamination of Commercial Cat Foods

Most of the contaminated pet foods that have been recalled over the past decade have been so, due to contaminated dry foods or treats. Dry cat foods contain high quantities of grains such as corn, wheat, oats, rice, and barley as well as soy which are commonly contaminated with molds, fungi, and bacteria. Contaminants such as aflatoxin from the fungus *Aspergillus sp.* and vomitoxin from the fungus *Fusarium sp.* are commonly found in these grains. Dry foods are typically the foods recalled with contamination of the bacteria *C. botulinum* (botulism) and *Salmonella sp*. Storage mites have also caused recalls of dry foods.

But, not only are biological contaminants dangerous so are chemical contaminants such as melamine and cyanuric acid which were responsible for the 2007 mass recalls which killed thousands of cats and dogs and made thousands of others terminally sick. Not only does this present a threat to your pet, it presents a threat to you and your family.

Inappropriate ingredient levels have also produced deadly foods such as recalls for lack of thiamin or toxic levels of zinc.

BHT & BHA

Preservatives such as BHT (butylated hydroxytoluene) and BHA (butylated hydroxyanisole) are used in food, cosmetics, rubber, and petroleum products. There is controversy surrounding their use in both human and animal foods as they are suspected of carcinogenicity. Many pet food companies now use mixed tocopherols from vitamin E.

Ethoxyquin

Another questionable preservative, mainly used to prevent oxidation of fish products, is ethoxyquin. It is associated with allergic reactions, skin problems, major organ failure, behavior problems, and cancer in dogs. However, there is little available scientific data to support those conclusions at this time. Nonetheless, the FDA/CVM has asked the pet food industry to voluntarily lower the maximum level of ethoxyquin in dog foods. Its effect on cats is unknown.

Selenium
Most dry and canned cat foods use an inorganic type of selenium – sodium selenite or sodium selenate. These forms of selenium are considered toxic by the National Toxicology Program of the US Department of Health and Human Services.[36]

Irradiation
Some pet food companies irradiate their food or food ingredients to sterilize the product. Irradiation of a certain cat food (in 2008) caused death in cats when it was found to be higher than the safe limits. The excessive irradiation caused destruction of much of the vitamin A in the food as well as increasing oxidation of the essential fatty acids DHA and EPA.[37] These two problems cause neurological symptoms and death is some affected cats.[38] This food was only sold in Australia. Australia required irradiation of pet foods with fresh meat or meat cooked at low temperatures, therefore only certain versions of the cat food and dog food were adulterated. In 2011, Australia banned irradiation of imported cat food. However, the dog food is still irradiated and some of the cats that fell ill only had access to the adulterated dog food.

Heavy Metals
Recent testing done on both cat and dog dry and wet foods (2011), has shown significant amounts of heavy metal contamination such as mercury, cadmium, arsenic, and beryllium.[39] Tuna has been notoriously cited as having high levels of mercury, therefore, tuna present in cat food may result in the food having high levels of mercury as well.

Bisphenol A (BPA)
Epoxy resins containing bisphenol A (BPA) are used as coatings on the inside of almost all food and beverage cans and can be toxic when it leaches into the food or drink. Experts as well as the FDA are working on further research into the human effects of BPA use. Suggested problems are fetal development, thyroid function, and cancer risk. Some plastics marked with the recycle codes 3 or 7 may contain BPA. A number of plastic container and bag manufacturers are now labeling their products BPA-free when the products lack this chemical.

Acidifiers
DL-methionine has been shown to cause Heinz body anemia in cats. Heinz bodies are small inclusions in red blood cells that result from the breakdown of hemoglobin. It is also suspect in the ever increasing condition known as idiopathic hypercalcemia. Acidifiers, mainly found in "urinary" formula diets may be in any maintenance diet, both dry and canned, or even in some treats. Other acidifiers commonly used are ammonium chloride, phosphoric acid, and sodium bisulfate. Acidifiers are also responsible for the increased occurrence of calcium oxalate stones.

Supplements
Through excessive processing and repeated high temperatures, many constituents of the original ingredients get destroyed. These components need to be added back in to the food at the end of processing. However, many of the ingredients added back in are synthetic versions of natural products or are not necessarily bioavailable such as iron from oxide/carbonate sources and copper from oxide sources. Pet foods are usually supplemented with essential trace minerals by way of inorganic salts. Organic proteinated or chelated substances (listed as such on the labels) are typically better tolerable and are easier for the cat's body to absorb. Trace mineral chelates have proven to be better than inorganic minerals in meeting the nutritional needs of cats.

Any food that contains antimicrobial or anti-vitamin compounds will cause depletion in the beneficial bacteria in the cat's intestines. This depletion will result in the loss of synthesis from bacteria colonies in the cat's intestine required for certain metabolic processes.

Vitamin K3
Menadione or synthetic vitamin K3 is often added to cat food. The FDA has banned its use in over-the-counter human supplements due to allergic reactions, hemolytic anemia, and cell toxicity in liver cells. The natural forms of vitamin K are vitamin K1 (phylloquinone from vegetable sources) and vitamin K2 (menaquinone from meat and eggs).

Onions & Garlic
Onions and garlic should always be avoided. They are in the genus *Allium* and both contain thiosulfate compounds which break down red blood cells and cause Heinz body anemia in cats.

Carrageenan
Carrageenan is made from seaweed and is used in canned food to help thicken and keep the food mixed. It has been associated with inflammation in dogs, cats, and humans, causes intestinal ulcers, and is a possible carcinogen. For cats with irritable bowel disease (IBD), this may cause complications.

GMOs (Genetically Modified Organisms)
GMOs are organisms that have had their DNA altered in order to produce a hardier plant that will resist insects, disease, drought, etc. GMOs have been shown to cause allergies and worse in humans and their effect on cats is unknown. High percentages of corn, soy, and some vegetable oils produced in the US are genetically modified.

Grains, Soy & Carbohydrates
Grains and carbohydrate sources should be eliminated or used sparingly. Many cases of IBD, diabetes, and obesity are resolved by switching cats to a grain-free, low-carbohydrate canned or raw diet. Soy has been shown to cause hyperthyroidism in humans and with the diagnosis of hyperthyroidism in cats; diet should be examined for soy products. Carbohydrates such as potatoes and peas are added to many high-protein grain-free canned diets. Carbohydrates should be restricted to no more than 10% of the daily caloric intake of your cat. However, less than 5% is ideal. Many dry cat foods contain in excess of 30% calories from carbohydrates.

Essential Fatty Acid Sources
Flaxseed oil is an effective source of essential fatty acids for humans. However, cats cannot get the full benefit of fatty acids from plant sources. Salmon oil or other fish body oil has a much higher bioavailability and digestibility for cats.

Non-Specified Source Ingredient
Ingredients listed as animal fat or meat meal should be avoided. Ingredients should identify the source of the protein such as chicken

fat or chicken meal. Non-specific protein sources may be any type of meat including horse, road kill, and even zoo animals.

Meat vs Meat By-Product
A muscle meat will be listed as chicken or turkey with no other qualifier.

Most by-products aren't as bad as they have been made out to be. Specified meat by-products (such as chicken by-products or beef by-products) are more nutritious than carbohydrates are for the cat. By-products are the rendered, clean parts, other than meat, derived from slaughtered mammals. It includes but is not limited to lungs, spleen, kidneys, brain, livers, blood, bone, partially defatted low temperature fatty tissue, and stomachs, and intestines freed of their contents. It does not include hair, horns, teeth, and hoofs.

Meal
Chicken meal is a muscle meat but the term meal denotes that it has been rendered (cooked for a long time at very high temperatures) and may be a lower quality product than just meat. A meal product or by-product is more commonly found in dry foods.

Yeast
Yeast ferments to alcohol and should be avoided. Yeast organisms may also produce waste products that can affect the immune system, nervous system, and endocrine system and can cause allergies, bladder infections, and skin disorders.

Vegetables & Fruit
These are added is some high-meat protein diets to appeal to humans. They also may relinquish some healthful nutrients. However, they are not necessary. As long as they do not contribute to more than 10% of overall carbohydrate daily calories, they are fine in small amounts.

Milk
Milk has also been seen as an ingredient in cat food. Most adult cats are lactose intolerant and milk, even in small quantities, may cause gastrointestinal problems such as bloating and diarrhea.

Ash
Ash is the inorganic residue remaining after the water and organic matter have been removed by heating. It is part of the dry matter and decreases the actual food calories if it is too high.

Water
Water in cat food is necessary for proper hydration, digestion, and urinary health. Water percentages should range from approximately 65-85% of the food. This obviously excludes all dry cat foods (and semi-moist foods). If you can make one change for your cat, feed your cat a wet diet only.

You can always add a little more water to a canned food if you think your cat needs it. Do not add water to dry kibble. Most dry foods contain mold and bacteria and they flourish in moisture.

Protein Sources
Chicken, turkey, and rabbit are the ideal main meat ingredients for cats. Beef may be used if your cat does not have a food allergy. Lamb is also a possibility since it is generally a novel (new) protein to your cat and may not produce allergic responses.

Keep in mind that your domestic cat evolved in the desert to eat small rodents, birds, insects, amphibians, and reptiles. Fish and beef are not natural proteins to a small desert cat. And both of these are typically allergenic in cats that are susceptible.

High quality chicken meat will sustain a cat longer than low quality plant-based protein that offers low bioavailability of nutrients to the cat. In this case, more food would need to be fed, thereby increasing your financial commitment. Please see Appendix E for a cost analysis.

Dry Food
If you must serve dry food to your cat during the transition stage from dry to wet, choose a grain-free, high-meat-protein food. This is a great addition when trying to convert your kibble (kitty crack) addicted cat to a wet diet. You can then phase out the dry food as your cat slowly converts. Many of these grain-free, high-meat-protein dry foods are too high in phosphorus and contraindicated in cats with renal disease or for long-term feeding.

Semi-Moist Food
These highly processed foods have higher moisture content than the dry varieties (10-12%) usually about 25-35%. However, the water content is still much too low and they are loaded with starches and sugars as well as alcohols to stabilize the food and prevent spoiling. Semi-moist foods should be completely avoided.

Canned Food
Canned cat foods contain anywhere from 65-80% moisture and are the most likely to contain higher percentages of meat protein as compared to dry foods. Calculating the values (see Chapter 11) of the ingredients, you can choose one that is high in meat protein with moderate fat and low carbohydrates. However, some canned cat foods, particularly the "therapeutic" variety may be high in carbohydrates such as corn and wheat. By reading labels, you'll notice that a brand of cat food may have dozens of "flavors", each with very different profiles, so reading each and every label is vital.

Raw Food
There are a number of commercial raw diets (65-85% moisture) now available in local pet shops and organic stores. These are great to feed your cat, but as with any commercial diet, make sure to read the labels carefully and if need be, work a few calculations. Many of the commercial raw diets contain fruits and vegetables (as well as some other questionable ingredients) which are neither required nor desired in a feline diet. Some are labeled as a supplement only, these would be added to an already balanced diet as a supplement or they themselves would need to be supplemented, for instance with liver and bone (bonemeal).

Commercial raw diets are great when converting a cat to a homemade raw food which is both healthier and cheaper to do yourself.

Treats & Snacks
Treats are not necessary to feed your cat. If you do wish to treat your cat, cooked or raw pieces of chicken breast are great snacks. For raw feeders, chicken gizzards are great for cats as well. Do not feed more than 10% of your cat's daily caloric intake as treats. Also, most commercial treats contain artificial dyes and preservatives. If you must

serve a commercial treat, look for ones with few ingredients and meat-based, such as some of the jerky-style treats.

Optimum Diet
Cats, as obligate carnivores, must eat a canned or raw diet high in meat protein with moderate fat and low carbohydrates for the best health benefits. There are a number of companies now producing canned and raw diets for cats that meet these criteria. Many still contain unnecessary ingredients such as starches (potatoes), vegetables, and fruits plus some questionable supplements. Care must be taken when reading and interpreting the labels.

From time to time, some companies change their ingredients. Make sure to always check the labels before purchasing to verify that the food is what you think it is and work in conjunction with your veterinarian.

Commercial Food Criteria
The following is a short list of requirements for a choosing a commercial cat food. If the commercial food in question meets the following criteria, then look for the quality of ingredients and question the company as to the source of those ingredients.

- Wet only diet – canned or raw
- Protein sources – chicken, turkey, rabbit, lamb (no beef or fish)
- Grain-free and soy-free
- Devoid of any of the questionable or deleterious ingredients listed in the previous pages of this chapter
- High meat protein - > 45% DMB, more than 50% is best
- Moderate fat - 25-35% DMB
- Low carbohydrate - <10% DMB, less than 5% is best

Benefits of a Canned Diet vs a Dry Diet
You may notice some of these changes immediately or it may take a few weeks to months for a positive outcome. It depends on the current health and physiology of your cat.

- Higher digestibility.

- Higher bioavailability.
- Less stool odor and better formed.
- Overweight cats will lose weight.
- Urine production will double due to proper hydration. Your cat will probably drink little to no water. However, keep fresh water available at all times.
- Dry, flaky skin and dull coat will disappear. Fur will become soft and glossy.
- Cats may become more energetic and playful.
- Some cats exhibit less shyness and exhibit more social interaction with other cats and people.
- Less vomiting and diarrhea. However, when a diet change is instituted, some cats may experience these symptoms for a week or two. Always proceed slowly when introducing new foods.
- Decrease of hairballs.
- BUN (blood urea nitrogen) a non-toxic by-product of protein metabolism, may be higher than the laboratories' safe range limits due to the high-meat-protein content of the food.
- Cats with urinary problems may see a marked improvement which may lead to complete remission without recurrence.
- Cats with IBD may see a marked improvement.
- Cats with diabetes will see a marked improvement which may lead to complete remission without recurrence. (only change your diabetic cat's diet with the assistance of your veterinarian – as blood sugar decreases, the insulin dose will also need to be decreased or a deadly condition of hypoglycemia may occur, usually within 24 hours).

13 – FEEDING, DAILY CALORIC INTAKE, & WEIGHT LOSS

Feeding Schedule
Small meals are metabolized rather quickly to allow the cat's body to be empty of food and waste so bacteria and parasites from their raw meat cannot reproduce. This is why cats often fast when they are not feeling well; fasting clears their systems.

Feeding ad libitum (ad lib) or free-choice causes a cat's digestive system to continue working nonstop and permits bacterial growth. Pressure is put on the kidneys, pancreas, liver, and intestines with no rest. Ad libitum feeding also tends to produce an alkaline situation making the regulation of the acid-base balance more difficult.

Recommended feedings are 2 to 4 per day for adult cats. Kittens and pregnant and lactating females should be fed at least four times per day. Choose a schedule that works both for you and your cat. Cats will typically adjust to any schedule especially if it is consistent. Small cats in the wild generally feed five to ten times per day. They eat small meals of mice, lizards, and even insects. In a domestic situation, adult cats can easily adapt to larger feedings less times per day.

Treats are not needed if you are feeding your cat an optimum diet. Raw food is digested more quickly and efficiently as compared to canned or cooked food. Dry food takes much longer to digest. If you must feed treats or are using food as a training mechanism, use some raw or

Feline Nutrition

cooked chicken breast. Treats should not exceed more than 10% of your cat's daily caloric intake.

Daily Caloric Intake

Many pet food companies that list the caloric content of the food on the packaging or on their websites, have grossly overestimated the quantity of the food to serve to domestic cats. For many cats, feeding these suggested amounts would actually cause weight gain. The following equations will help you determine, approximately, how many calories you should feed your cat per day, this may vary by sex, sterilization, activity level, size, and lifestage (kitten, junior, mature, senior, geriatric, pregnant, and lactating).

This is a generalization so that you have a basic idea of the daily caloric intake of a domestic cat. General feeding guidelines should be adjusted up or down to maintain the ideal body weight and body condition of your cat.

12 pound cat maintaining its weight
(13.6 Calories x 12 pounds) + 70 = **233 Calories (kcal) per day**

Switching cats to a high-meat-protein/low-carbohydrate canned or raw diet will produce weight loss in overweight or obese cats without having to increase physical activity. However, as weight loss continues, physical activity will increase, as well, assisting in further weight loss.

To calculate what your cat should be consuming when losing weight:
16 pound cat that needs to lose weight to become 12 pounds
12 pounds x 15 Calories = **180 Calories (kcal) per day minimum**

Most cats will eat about 4 to 5 ounces of canned or raw food per day, based on average caloric content.

Weight Loss

If your cat is losing weight, make sure it does not lose more than 1-2% of its body weight per week. If your cat is losing too much weight too quickly, feed more food. Adding some raw or cooked chicken meat will also help raise the protein level of the food without adding too much fat. Keep this below 10% of daily caloric intake.

Calculating Percent Body Weight
12 pound cat
Convert pounds to ounces first (16oz in a pound)
12 pounds x 16 ounces = 192 ounces

1% of 192 ounces
192 oz x .01 = 1.92 ounces per week weight loss

2% of 192 ounces
192 oz x .02 = 3.84 ounces per week weight loss

Your 12 pound cat should not lose more than about 1.9-3.8 ounces per week.

To help monitor weight loss, purchase an electronic baby scale to weigh your cat twice weekly in the initial stages of weight loss and a few times yearly thereafter to monitor his weight (see Appendix A). Monitoring weight loss is important, particularly in overweight or obese cats. If weight loss progresses too quickly, your cat may stop eating, causing fat to accumulate in the liver (hepatic lipidosis) leading to an emergency situation. Cats should not go more than 24 hours without eating.

Veterinarian Support
When changing your cat's diet, you should always consult your veterinarian first. Blood work should be done to make sure your cat is in good enough condition for the change. Diabetic and obese cats are at the most risk of problems when making a diet change. Diabetic cats may go into hypoglycemic shock when reducing carbohydrates while still administering the regular insulin dose and overweight cats may stop eating, leading to fast weight loss and hepatic lipidosis.

14 – HOMEMADE RAW CAT FOOD

It is important to remember that you must attain blood work (complete blood count and chemistry profile) for your cat before any diet change, to make sure your cat will not have any adverse effects from the conversion. Speak to your veterinarian so he/she may address any concerns. This diet is not recommended for cats that have chronic renal disease (see Appendix A for more help).

If you wish to make a homemade diet for your cat(s), use only a *raw* food recipe. Cooking the diet will destroy many of the required nutrients and you will be serving a less than balanced diet. If you would prefer to serve a cooked food, purchase a quality canned food. Commercially produced raw food is also available. However, making raw food for your cat will be more cost effective than purchasing it and you will have absolute control of the ingredients used.

The recipes below are based on Natascha Wille's, initial recipe for raw cat food, distributed since 1997.[40] These recipes or ones similar to them have been fed for years, worldwide. Veering too far from these appropriately balanced recipes may be detrimental to your cat. Ingredients that are optional, if your cat has an aversion to them or has problems digesting them, will be noted.

The recipes below are the ones that Dr. Lisa Pierson (of catinfo.org) uses with slight modifications.

The only recipes offered are made with ground bone. There really is no substitute for fresh ground bone. It is also important to note that *cooked* bone can splinter and is very dangerous to cats. However, *raw* ground bone is easily digested by carnivores.

If you are taking on the task of making a homemade raw diet, you might as well buy a grinder and use bone with the recipe. There are a number of reasons to do it this way:

- Pre-ground meat has the surface bacteria already ground into it.
- The pre-ground meat is often placed in the display case at the store for an unspecified amount of time, allowing bacteria to grow.
- The butchers that prepared the ground meat expect that the consumer will be cooking it, so, their equipment and/or handling procedures may not be as sanitary in its preparation.

If you are converting a dry-fed feline over to a wet diet, it may be wise to convert them to a canned or commercial raw diet before introducing them to a homemade diet. Conversion can sometimes be a long process with cats and you shouldn't get discouraged to the point of giving up. Give yourself and your cat time to adjust to the new diet. One quick way of introduction would be to thoroughly rinse a chicken breast and cut it up into small bite-size pieces to see if your cat is already interested in this natural diet.

Protein Sources – Main Ingredient
These recipes call for chicken thighs but whole chickens can be used as well. When using whole chickens, remove the necks and backbones to reduce the amount of bone or the calcium-phosphorus ratio may be compromised.

Beef and fish have been shown to be hyperallergenic in the cat and raw fish should never be fed because it contains thiaminase which will lead to a thiamin (vitamin B1) deficiency in the cat. Fish also tends to be addictive to cats because of the strong scent and taste. Certain species of fish, such as tuna, may be contaminated with heavy metals such as mercury. Fish is also high in magnesium which may cause a problem for cats that already have or are prone to urinary problems.

Grain-fed beef is also higher in fat, lower in protein, and usually loaded with antibiotics and growth hormones than grass-fed and/or organically raised cattle. Bovine spongiform encephalitis (BSE – mad cow disease) may also be spread to cats in the form of feline spongiform encephalitis (FSE).

Pork is not recommended. Trichinosis is caused by eating raw pork that is contaminated with the larvae of the roundworm *Trichinella spp*. Pork is also extremely high in fat and is no substitution for small rodents and birds.

Additional meats that can be used are Cornish game hens, quail, turkey, or rabbit. The turkey bones will not go through the grinder as is, without first being broken into smaller pieces.

Tips
There are two separate recipes, one with chicken only and one with rabbit and chicken. The reasons for the rabbit and chicken combination are threefold: chicken is much cheaper than rabbit, the rabbit has a higher bone to meat ratio, and the rabbit is leaner than chicken. So, by adding in some chicken meat and skin, the bone to meat ratio is lowered and the fat is increased.

It is best to use organic, free-range, antibiotic-free chicken and eggs. Whatever best fits your financial situation is appropriate. Currently, there are no FDA approved growth hormones for poultry, therefore, all poultry in the United States is hormone-free.

Chicken hearts are sometimes hard to source, especially in the quantities needed if you make large batches of food. In this case, taurine is substituted. Check with your local butcher or large grocery store chain. They may be able to source the hearts for you if you give them a few days notice each time you need them. Ethnic food stores are also a good place to check as they typically offer foods not offered in the traditional grocery stores.

You'll notice that chunking much of the meat is suggested, providing some dental health benefit. Using poultry shears works much better than a knife. However, if your cat will not eat the chunks, grind all of the meat instead.

For most meat grinders, including the one listed in Appendix D, it is best to wash all parts by hand to prevent rusting. Use the 4mm (5/32") grind plate for grinding.

If you will be freezing your cat food for more than two weeks, you may wish to sprinkle a little extra taurine and salmon oil on your cat's food when serving, one or two of the meals per week. Both of these ingredients may deteriorate in prolonged freezing conditions. It is well known that taurine is sensitive to both grinding and freezing and essential fatty acids in the salmon oil are also sensitive to oxidation.

It takes me two hours to make 25 pounds of food including packaging and cleanup. I make food every three weeks.

Make sure to wash your hands well before beginning and use only clean utensils and bowls.

Chicken Only Recipe

Ingredients:
4.5 pounds chicken thighs including bones and skin
14 oz chicken hearts (if not using – add 14 oz meat/bones to recipe and add 4000 mg taurine)
7 oz chicken livers
2 cups water
4 egg yolks (raw egg whites contain avidin which depletes biotin)
4000 mg wild salmon oil (never cod liver oil)
200 mg vitamin B complex
800 IU vitamin E
1.5 teaspoons lite iodized salt
4000 mg taurine additionally, if freezing for more than a week.

Directions:
1. Remove half of the skin and 20% of the bones from the chicken thighs and discard.
2. Rinse the meat, under cold running water, to remove surface bacteria.

3. Chunk up most of the muscle meat with poultry shears.
4. Grind the rest of the muscle meat, bones, skin, heart, and liver. Stir well.
5. Measure two cups of water into a bowl and whisk in the egg yolks, salmon oil, vitamin B complex, vitamin E, lite iodized salt, and added taurine (if using in place of hearts and/or adding because of freezing).
6. Mix the chunked meat, ground mixture, and supplement mixture together.
7. Fill containers. Leave room in the containers for expansion from freezing. Mark the containers with both the contents and date and freeze.

Makes approximately 6¼ pounds (100 oz).
Cats eat about 4-5 ounces per day.
This recipe is not recommended for cats with chronic renal disease.

Rabbit & Chicken Combo

Ingredients:
3¾ pounds ground rabbit (ground rabbit typically includes the meat/bones/head which includes the heart, liver, and thyroid gland – check with your supplier)
¾ pound chicken thigh meat and skin (no bone)
14 oz chicken hearts (if not using – add 14 oz chicken meat/bones to recipe and add 4000 mg taurine)
0 or 7 oz chicken livers (if the ground rabbit contains liver – do not add)
2 cups water
4 egg yolks (raw egg whites contain avidin which depletes biotin)
4000 mg wild salmon oil (never cod liver oil)
200 mg vitamin B complex
800 IU vitamin E
0 or 1.5 teaspoons lite iodized salt (if the ground rabbit contains the thyroid gland – do not add)
4000 mg taurine additionally, if freezing for more than a week

Directions:
1. Rinse the meat, under cold running water, to remove surface bacteria.
2. Chuck up most of the chicken muscle meat with poultry shears.

3. Grind the rest of the chicken muscle meat, skin, liver (if using), and heart (if using) and add to ground rabbit. Stir well.
4. Measure two cups of water into a bowl and whisk in the egg yolks, salmon oil, vitamin B complex, vitamin E, lite iodized salt (if using), and added taurine (if using in place of hearts and/or adding because of freezing).
5. Mix the chunked meat, ground mixture and supplement mixture together.
6. Fill containers. Leave room in the containers for expansion from freezing. Mark the containers with both the contents and date and freeze.

Makes approximately 6¼ pounds (100 oz).
Cats eat about 4-5 ounces per day.
This recipe is not recommended for cats with chronic renal disease.

Explanation of Ingredients
The following is an explanation of the ingredients used in the recipes above. Please do not alter these recipes as the ingredients are carefully balanced. Optional ingredients are noted.

Certain nutrients including many vitamins and amino acids are degraded by the temperatures, pressures, and chemical treatments used during the manufacture of commercial cat foods and must be added after manufacturing to avoid nutritional deficiency. Grinding and freezing a homemade diet has also shown that some nutrients, specifically taurine, may be degraded by these processes. Supplementation of certain nutrients is therefore necessary in the homemade diet as well.

One must also take into consideration that natural prey would eat natural grasses and seeds. Prey is high in omega-3 fatty acids, protein, and vitamin E and lower in fat than commercially raised grain-fed poultry and beef, therefore, supplements are added to balance out these deficiencies or excesses.

Chicken Thigh Meat
Chicken thighs supply vitamin K and are a good source of vitamin B6, vitamin D, pantothenic acid, phosphorus, zinc, and selenium, and a very good source of protein, niacin, and fat.[41]

Chicken thigh is higher in taurine and fat and cheaper than chicken breast so it is the best cut of poultry to use if you are not using the whole carcass. Amino acids are the building blocks of tissue and are necessary for the proper formation of skin, hair, muscles, and the cells that make up many other organ systems.

Phosphorus, like calcium, plays a major role in the development and maintenance of bones and teeth but also plays an important role in cell metabolism. Phosphorus from animal sources and mineral supplements are usually completely available. Meat in the diet provides an excellent source of phosphorus.

Vitamin D helps the body utilize calcium and phosphorus and is critical in the formation and maintenance of bones and teeth. Cats cannot synthesize vitamin D from sunlight and therefore must receive their vitamin D through dietary means.

Selenium has a variety of functions. It helps make special proteins, called antioxidant enzymes, which play a role in preventing cell damage. It works with vitamin E as an antioxidant and immunostimulator. Because of its strong ability to stimulate the immune system, it is the most effective defense against some viral infections.

L-lysine occurs naturally in raw meat and is used as a supplemental treatment for the herpes virus common in cats.

Co-enzyme Q10 (ubiquinone), a fat soluble, vitamin-like substance, supports brain, liver, kidney, and heart function and is found naturally in meat, heart, and liver.

Bones, Chicken
Supplies calcium, phosphorus, magnesium, copper, and zinc.

About half of bone is made of a carbonated form of hydroxylapatite or calcium apatite. The primary role of calcium is building bones and teeth and almost all of the calcium in a cat's body is used to build these two structures. Bones in the diet provide an excellent source of calcium. Bones also contain magnesium, manganese, boron, silica, phosphorus, fluoride, sodium, potassium, copper, and zinc. Chicken thigh and breast meats are naturally low in copper and zinc so bone is also required for these two minerals. Bone contains collagen, a fibrous protein also found in the skin, cartilage, and tendons, which provides structural support and strength to the cells that comprise them.

Magnesium is an essential mineral. It is involved in numerous functions of the body like energy production, formation of urea, muscle relaxation, and neuromuscular transmission and activity.

Skin, Chicken
This skin is a good source of fat and also supplies vitamin K.[42]

Like protein, fats serve as an energy source. Compared to carbohydrates and proteins, fats are a much more concentrated form of dietary energy, providing more than twice the calories and energy. Fats also supply the essential fatty acids linoleic acid and arachidonic acid. Fats aid in the absorption of the fat soluble vitamins A, D, E, and K and make the food more palatable to cats. Arachidonic acid is only found in animal fats.

Heart, Chicken
Chicken hearts are a good source of niacin, vitamin B6, folate, pantothenic acid, phosphorus and copper, and a very good source of protein, riboflavin, vitamin B12, fat, iron, zinc, and taurine.[43]

Heart can sometimes be very hard to source. Check with local small butchers and specialty shops for a supply. If you can't find it, make sure to replace the recipe amount, for example 14 oz of heart to be replaced with 14 oz of chicken meat with bone and 4000 mg of taurine.

Co-enzyme Q10 (ubiquinone), a fat soluble, vitamin-like substance, supports brain, liver, kidney, and heart function and is found naturally in meat, heart, and liver.

Liver, Chicken
Liver is a good source of thiamin, zinc, manganese, and fat, and a very good source of protein, vitamin A, vitamin C, vitamin D, riboflavin, niacin, vitamin B6, vitamin B12, pantothenic acid, iron, phosphorus, copper and selenium.[44]

The nervous system and the heart are particularly sensitive to thiamin deficiency, because of their high oxidative metabolism. In the cat, a lack of thiamin can be caused by a diet high in thiaminase-rich foods such as raw fish.

The primary functions of vitamin A are helping maintain proper eyesight, helping maintain normal healthy skin, and bone and tooth metabolism. Vitamin A occurs naturally, only in animal tissues. While omnivores and herbivores can convert beta-carotene (from plants) to vitamin A, cats cannot because they lack the proper enzyme to do so.

Copper, a mineral, is necessary (along with iron) for the formation of hemoglobin. It also helps keep bones, blood vessels, and nerves healthy.

Although cats possess the enzymes needed for niacin synthesis, the high activity of enzymes in the catabolic pathway prevents niacin synthesis. As a result, niacin is required in large amounts in the cat's diet.

Water
Supplies moisture.

Water is the most essential nutrient of survival for the cat. Without water, death can occur in as little as a few days. Water supplies moisture to the diet to aide in dispersal of the supplements. Water is an excellent solvent and helps absorb excess heat and slowly distribute it throughout the body.

Egg Yolks, Chicken (Optional)
Egg yolks supply vitamin K and are a good source of protein, folate, vitamin B12, vitamin D, and phosphorus, and a very good source of fat and selenium.[45]

Eggs are a concentrated way to increase protein in the diet. They also supply many additional vitamins and minerals. Raw egg whites contain avidin which depletes biotin in the body requiring them to be cooked prior to feeding, therefore, only egg yolks are used in this raw recipe.

Taurine
Supplied by hearts or as a supplement.

Cats are unable to manufacture taurine themselves, and must therefore receive it from their diet. Taurine has been shown to degrade quickly upon processing such as grinding and freezing. These recipes call for additional supplementation of taurine to combat that.

Vitamin B Complex (Optional)
Vitamin B Complex usually contains thiamin, riboflavin, niacin, pantothenic acid, pyridoxine, cobalamin, folic acid, and biotin. It is supplied by meat, organs, and supplementation in these diets. It is for eye, heart, skin, and nerve health. Cats require high levels of all of these B vitamins. The B vitamins also protect against disease and viruses. Vitamin B12 (cobalamin) is only found in meat products while the rest are found in plants, meat, and liver.

Vitamin E
Vitamin E (d-alpha-tocopherol) is a fat-soluble antioxidant that stops the oxidation of fat. Vitamin E supplementation is needed when adding fatty acids (salmon oil) and fat (chicken skin) to prevent rancidity. Purchasing vitamin E in a dry capsule form is less messy to use and it stays fresh longer.

Wild Salmon Oil (Fish Body Oil)
Supplies omega-3 fatty acids. Do not substitute cod liver oil for salmon oil.

Cod *liver* oil contains large quantities of vitamins A and D. These additional amounts could prove toxic when using chicken liver in this recipe. You may use any fish body oil such as salmon, sardine, or anchovy, however salmon is the best source with the highest quantity of omega-3 fatty acids. Next would be menhaden, sardine, and then herring.

Fish body oil supplies essential fatty acids which are supplied by brains and eyes. The salmon oil listed in Appendix D has high levels of EPA (eicosapentaenoic acid) and DHA (docosahexaenoic acid), omega-3 polyunsaturated fatty acids (PUFAs). Extended storage has shown a decrease in essential fatty acid activity. Salmon oil is best purchased as individual capsules. Once fish oil has been exposed to the air, it will turn rancid quickly. The capsules prevent this from happening.

Feline Nutrition

The use of wild fish body oil is higher in both EPA found in the tissues of prey eating algae and DHA found in the sperm, brains, and retinas of their prey.

Salt, Lite Iodized
Lite iodized salt supplies iodine for meat mixtures lacking the thyroid gland as well as potassium and sodium. Iodine is necessary for the proper functioning of the thyroid gland and the production of thyroid hormones. Thyroid hormones regulate the rate of metabolism in the body and play an important role in normal growth.

Nutrient Analysis
Although there is not currently a nutrient profile of the homemade raw diet, the following table lists the basic nutrients of a rat carcass. As you can see, high (meat) protein, moderate fat, and low carbohydrates would be on the menu of a wild-fed cat.

Table 4: Nutrient profile of a rat carcass.[46]

Nutrient *	Rat Carcass
Moisture	63.6%
Protein	55%
Fat	38.1%
Carbohydrate	1.2%
Fiber	0.55%
Ash	5.22%
Calcium	1.15%
Phosphorus	0.98%
Magnesium	0.08%
Linoleic Acid	9.1%
Iron	288 mg/kg
Vitamin A	84,800 IU/kg
Niacin	156.6 mg/kg

*All nutrients expressed on a dry matter basis except moisture.

Storage
Raw food may be stored in plastic containers available from your local grocer. You may also wish to use freezer specific glass jars. Another method is to vacuum seal the contents in plastic or use zipper type freezer bags. The most important issue is making sure that the storage

container is rated for freezer use. Also, if at all possible, only use BPA-free plastic.

The food must be kept frozen until it needs to be thawed. If you do not have enough space in your kitchen freezer, you may need to purchase an additional small freezer or make smaller batches of food. Small freezers are available at large department stores, home improvement stores, and appliance stores.

This raw food diet should not be stored more than a couple of months in the freezer. Extended storage may lead to the breakdown of most if not all of the taurine and there could be a decrease in essential fatty acid activity and destruction of vitamin E. Freezing this diet for a minimum of 48 hours (when first made) before serving may help kill some to all of the parasites (not bacteria – they become dormant) that may be in the food.

If you live in an area that experiences frequent and lengthy power outages, you may need a portable generator. Make sure to follow the directions for the generator, as it produces invisible and deadly carbon monoxide fumes. Used correctly, they are safe and handy to have.

Thawing & Feeding
Calculate the approximate amount to feed each cat per day (see Chapter 13). Most cats eat about 4-6 ounces per day. Then calculate the total amount you will be feeding per day and place that amount in the refrigerator to thaw, at least 24 hours before. Smaller packages will thaw more quickly so you may opt to split a daily serving into two smaller containers. Larger containers may take up to 48 hours to thaw. You should not leave thawed meat in the fridge more than 48-72 hours after thawing, before using or discarding.

Plates are easier for cats to eat from than bowls. Small plates allow cats to put their heads down without interfering with their whiskers. When eating small prey, cats' whiskers are held straight out from their faces. When cats try to eat from a bowl, their whiskers are forced backwards, which for some cats may prove bothersome, causing them to walk away from the food.

Feeding two to three meals per day is suggested. Leave the food down for no more than 30 minutes and then take away any leftovers. You may cover the food and return it to the refrigerator to try later and then discard it. Never place food that has been served back into the original container.

Kittens will eat more than adult cats and seniors will eat less. Kittens should be fed several times a day to keep up with their active metabolisms and growing bodies. Whether feeding kittens, adults, seniors, or pregnant or lactating queens, the recipe is the same. However, this recipe is not recommended for cats with kidney disease. Please see Appendix A for more help with CRD cats.

Thawing Raw Food in a Pinch
If you forgot to thaw the food out or need to quick-thaw food that is not completely thawed, put the food to be thawed in a plastic baggie and zip it closed tightly. Float the bag in a bowl of *cold* tap water for about 30 minutes or until thawed. You may change the water out after 15 minutes with *cold* tap water again. It is imperative you do not use warm or hot water. Meat may be heated in warm water for serving but not for thawing. The heat will activate any bacteria that may be present in the food.

Warming & Serving the Raw Diet
Take the serving of thawed food from the refrigerator and transfer it to a zipper type baggie. Press it flat then zip it closed tightly. Let it soak in warm water, in a shallow bowl, for a minute or so then replace the water with warm water again and flip the bag to the other side for another minute. This will heat it up a bit. Cats prefer their food at mouse body temperature (98°F) but room temperature works just fine.

You may also opt to remove the raw food from the refrigerator about 30 minutes before serving. This method is fine, if when served, it is eaten right away.

It seems no one agrees on whether microwaves damage the amino acids, vitamins, and minerals in the food when heating. I have been unable to find any definitive sources that agree one way or another, so to be safe, always warm the food in a water bath and never microwave it.

Safety & Handling of a Raw Diet
Your cat evolved to eat its food raw and makes efficient use of the nutrients in a raw diet for optimum health.

A raw food diet is the most natural of all diets to feed the feline. "The *Campylobacter* and *Salmonella* organisms present on chicken skin are well tolerated by the gastrointestinal tract of kittens and cats, but owners should wash their hands well after meal preparation."[47]

Cats in the wild often drag their food up trees or bury it to save for a later meal. Food poisoning is always a possibility, but with proper handling as you would with any meat product you would prepare for yourself or your family, cats may be fed a high quality raw diet safely.

Cat saliva contains an enzyme called lysozyme, which attacks bacteria as it enters the mouth by digesting the coating of the bacteria. Any remaining contaminants enter the cat's extremely short and acidic intestinal tract. A cat's short digestive transit time, as compared to other carnivores and omnivores, prevents the remaining pathogens in the gut to grow before they are evacuated from the body.

It is always important to follow safety protocol when working with raw meat. Food dishes, countertops, and feeding areas, as well as hands should be washed before and after working with the raw meat. Disinfect the area where you prepared or fed your cats, even if it looks clean. A bleach solution (1:22 bleach/water) or distilled white vinegar followed by a 3% hydrogen peroxide solution are the cheapest, easiest, and safest to use around cats for disinfection. Your home will not smell like vinegar since the smell dissipates in seconds as the vinegar dries.

As with any possible pathogen, the young, elderly, and people with compromised immune systems should handle raw meat and foods carefully. This is also necessary when feeding dry food, as most dry foods are contaminated with fungi, bacteria, and molds.

Treats & Snacks

When using a raw diet, treats or snacks are not needed. A raw diet is an optimum diet for cats and no other supplementation is required. If need be, you may opt to give raw chicken gizzards or some chunks of raw chicken breast as a snack or training aid. Chunks of raw chicken breast are also good for cats with few or no teeth. The chunks of meat are easy to swallow whole, as most cats eat that way anyway. Just don't make the pieces too big.

Benefits of a Raw Diet

You may notice some of these changes immediately or it may take a few weeks to months for a positive outcome. It depends on the current health and physiology of your cat.

- High digestibility.
- High bioavailability.
- No odor from the food.
- No stool odor and stool will be well-formed.
- Adult cats may only defecate every other day. Stool will be light in color and dry and crumbly.
- Overweight cats will lose weight.
- Underweight cats will gain weight.
- Normal weight cats will add muscle tone.
- Urine production will double due to proper hydration. Your cat will probably drink little to no water. However, keep fresh water available at all times.
- Dry, flaky skin and dull coat will disappear. Fur will become soft and glossy.
- Cats may become more energetic and playful.
- Some cats exhibit less shyness and exhibit more social interaction with other cats and people.
- Less vomiting and diarrhea. However, when a diet change is instituted, some cats may experience these symptoms for a week or two.
- Decrease of hairballs.
- BUN (blood urea nitrogen) a non-toxic by-product of protein metabolism, may be higher than the laboratories' safe range limits due to the high-meat-protein content of the food.

- Cats with urinary problems may see a marked improvement which may lead to complete remission without recurrence.
- Cats with IBD may see a marked improvement which may lead to complete remission without recurrence.
- Cats with diabetes will see a marked improvement which may lead to complete remission without recurrence. (only change your diabetic cat's diet with the assistance of your veterinarian – as blood sugar decreases, the insulin dose will also need to be decreased or a deadly condition of hypoglycemia may occur usually within 24 hours).

How to Approach Your Veterinarian Concerning a Raw Diet

Many veterinarians that are concerned about clients feeding their cats a raw diet stem from their experiences of treating cats that have been fed unbalanced home-prepared diets.

Infection from pathogenic bacteria such as *Salmonella sp.* or *E. coli* in healthy cats fed a raw diet is undocumented at this time. However, many cats have presented with deficiencies or toxicities due to overzealous owners getting artistic with already balanced recipes or trying to formulate one from scratch. It is of the utmost importance that you do not alter these balanced recipes unless you specifically seek out your veterinarian's or feline nutritionist's expertise on the subject.

When approaching your veterinarian, bring a copy of the diet so he/she may review it and discuss with you any concerns or changes they feel are necessary for your individual cat's needs. Many veterinarians are more than willing to help you achieve optimum nutrition for your cat. Having a starting point, such as the recipes included here, will allow for open communication. Your veterinarian may also wish to keep the recipe to review at length or for consultation with an animal nutritionist for more information.

15 – SWITCHING YOUR CAT TO A WET DIET

Switching your cat to a canned or raw diet may prove challenging. Some cats will take to canned/raw food very quickly, especially when they have already been fed some canned food on a regular basis. However, many cats switching from a completely dry food to canned will fight tooth and nail for their dry kibble. With persistence, most cats will make the switch between a few days to a few weeks, however, extremely stubborn individuals may take a few months. One of my cats took four months to switch from a dry/canned diet to a canned only diet. He was obese at the time and required twice weekly weigh-ins. His refusal of food on many occasions was exceedingly frustrating but by using some of the methods below he was able to make the transition, all the while losing weight at a safe pace. He is now a normal weight, homemade raw fed cat.

Diabetic cats that are switched to a high meat protein, low carbohydrate wet food, will oftentimes no longer need insulin injections. For those that do still need insulin, the doses are typically minimal. Please work in conjunction with your veterinarian on any diet change. These cats often need their insulin dose decreased within a day or two of beginning this type of diet. If their insulin dose is not evaluated, they could become hypoglycemic which could lead to death. For more information and a treatment protocol for your veterinarian to follow, please see Appendix A.

Overweight and obese cats and cats that are poor eaters should be monitored closely while undergoing this transition. Cats should not lose more than 1-2% of their body weight per week and no cat should go longer than 24 hours without eating.

These particular raw diets are not recommended for cats with chronic renal disease. Please see Appendix A for more information.

Tips for Making the Switch
- Stop feeding free-choice (ad lib) and develop a feeding schedule that works for you and your cat. Two to four meals per day are suggested. Your cats will learn the schedule and also finish their portions in the allotted time when they adjust to this new feeding format.
- Choose several canned foods to begin with, representing different types of flavors and textures including some pâté styles and chunk and gravy styles to see which version your cat is more interested in trying. Usually the odiferous fish scented ones work best for most cats and many have high meat by-product content and low carbohydrates that will appeal to cats. They are good for the short-term transition before transitioning to a better quality canned or raw food.
- Some grain-free, high-meat-protein dry foods may also be used to entice your cats to try the canned food by mixing it into the food and sprinkling some pieces on top. However, these are not to be used forever as they still lack sufficient water for the cat's diet and many are too high in phosphorus.
- Slowly, over several days or weeks, reduce the amount of dry food and increase the amount of wet.
- You may also add low-sodium tuna water, low-sodium chicken broth (no onions or garlic), some cooked chicken chunks, or meat only baby food (no onions or garlic) to the canned food. Drizzle some of the canned food juice or gravy over the canned food to make it more enticing.
- Start a play session about ten or fifteen minutes before you plan on feeding. In the wild, cats would have to chase down their prey before eating, thereby working up an appetite.
- Whenever a dietary change occurs the gastrointestinal tract may need time to adjust to the new diet. Some cats may experience

softer stools or diarrhea. That is why it is important to go slowly with this process. Some cats will regurgitate after eating as well. If this happens, slow the process down.
- You may be throwing away a lot of uneaten food during this transitional phase.
- Don't Give Up! This may be a lesson in frustration but not in futility!

Switching your cat to a wet, grain-free, high-meat-protein, moderate-fat, low-carbohydrate diet is the single best thing you can ever do for your cat. Not only your cat, but you will reap the benefits; your cat will enjoy excellent health and longevity and you will rest easy knowing you have given your cat the best nutrition you could while also saving money on veterinary expenses.

APPENDIX A
USEFUL WEBSITES AND INFORMATION

Dr. Lisa Pierson – http://catinfo.org
For information about feline nutrition and a raw food diet.

Dr. Lisa Pierson – drpierson@catinfo.org
To request a phone consultation for a diet for chronic kidney disease in cats. All consultations are conducted via the telephone (or Skype) only after the patient's medical records, including lab work, have been provided for her review. General CRD medical management to prolong the length and quality of life, in addition to appropriate dietary issues, is discussed during the consultation. Her CRD consultations take up approximately 2 hours of phone time since there is a lot to discuss if optimal CRD management is desired.

Dr. Elizabeth Hodgkins – http://yourdiabeticcat.com
For information about diabetic cat care and a treatment protocol for your veterinarian to follow.

FDA Safety Reporting Portal – to report a pet food complaint.
Make sure to report the pet food complaint to your State Department of Agriculture as well.

http://www.fda.gov/AnimalVeterinary/SafetyHealth/ReportaProblem/ucm182403.htm

Electronic Baby Scale – Salter 914 Electronic Baby and Toddler Scale weighs up to 44 pounds (20 kg) at half-ounce increments (10 g) and features a hold button so you can get an accurate weight, even from a moving cat. It is available at Amazon.com.

APPENDIX B
NUTRITIONAL CALCULATIONS

Percentage Calculations

For example, to remove 20% of the bones from the chicken thighs:
Chicken thigh count = 65
65 x .20% = 13
13 thigh bones should be removed from the 65 thighs.

Calcium to Phosphorus to Magnesium Ratio
Ca = 0.513%
P = 0.360%
Mg = 0.025%

To figure out the ratio, make sure the minerals have the same units, either percentage or in milligrams (mg).
Divide the calcium by the phosphorus: 0.513/0.360 = 1.43
Divide the magnesium by the phosphorus: 0.025/0.360 = 0.07
Calcium-phosphorus-magnesium ratio is 1.43:1:0.07

Daily Caloric Intake

12 pound cat maintaining its weight
(13.6 calories x 12 pounds) + 70 = *233 calories (kcal) per day*

16 pound cat that needs to lose weight to become 12 pounds
12 pounds x 15 calories = *180 calories (kcal) per day minimum*

Percent Body Weight
A cat should not lose more than 1-2% of its body weight per week.

12 pound cat
Convert pounds to ounces first (16oz/pound):
12 pounds x 16 ounces = 192 ounces

1% of 192 ounces
192 x .01 = 1.92 ounces per week weight loss

Appendix B

2% of 192 ounces
192 x .02 = 3.84 ounces per week weight loss
Between 1.9 and 3.8 oz per week weight loss is safe for a 12 pound cat.

Calculating the DMB (Dry Matter Basis)
when comparing wet to dry

Dry Food		*Canned Food*	
Protein	36%	Protein	10%
Fat	18%	Fat	5%
Moisture	11%	Moisture	78%

Dry Food Protein = 36%
Dry Food Moisture = 11%
100% (dry and wet) – 11% (wet) = 89% dry
(36% Protein / 89% dry) x 100 = *40% Protein DMB in dry food*

Canned Food Protein = 10%
Canned Food Moisture = 78%
100% (dry and wet) – 78% (wet) = 22% dry
(10% Protein / 22% dry) x 100 = *45% Protein DMB in canned food*

Calculating Nutrient Percentages

1. Calculate the Percentage of Food Weight

To calculate the approximate weight of the carbohydrate in a food, add up the values for protein, fat, moisture, fiber, and ash and subtract this value from 100%.

As Fed Values per 100 grams

Protein	10%
Fat	5%
Moisture	78%
Fiber	1%
Ash	1.95%

10 + 5 + 78 + 1 + 1.95 = 95.95%

Feline Nutrition

100% - 95.95% = *4.05% Carbohydrate Weight*

2. Calculate the Percentage of Dry Matter Weight

Dry Matter Basis removes the water from the equation.
Convert 4.05% Carbohydrate Weight to DMB
100% (dry and wet) - 78% (wet) = 22% dry
(4.05% Carbohydrate / 22% dry) x 100 = *18% Carbohydrate DMB*

3. Calculate the Percentage of Calories

This is the best method for comparing values.
A cat should not receive more than 10% of their daily dietary calories from carbohydrates, less than 5% is better.

Protein and Carbohydrates contribute 4 calories per gram.
Fat contributes 9 calories per gram.

For conversion, you may use either the GA values or the AF values. Whichever method you choose to use for the calculations, make sure to remain consistent with all values. AF values are more accurate.

As Fed Values per 100 grams

Protein	10%
Fat	5%
Moisture	78%
Fiber	1%
Ash	1.95%
Carbohydrate	4.05%

10g Protein x 4 Calories = 40 Calories Protein
5 g Fat x 9 Calories = 45 Calories Fat
4.05 g Carbohydrate x 4 Calories = 16.2 Calories Carbohydrates

40 Calories Protein + 45 Calories Fat + 16.2 Calories Carbohydrates = 101.2 Calories per 100 grams of food (≈3.5 ounces)

To calculate the percentage we must divide the calories for each nutrient by the total calories in 100 grams of food:
(40 Calories of Protein / 101.2 Calories) x 100 = *39.5% Calories from Protein*
(45 Calories of Fat / 101.2 Calories) x 100 = *44.5% Calories from Fat*

Appendix B

(16.2 Calories of Carbohydrates / 101.2 Calories) x 100 = *16% Calories from Carbohydrates*

APPENDIX C
RAW CAT FOOD RECIPES

Chicken Only Recipe
Ingredients:
4.5 pounds chicken thighs including bones and skin
14 oz chicken hearts (if not using – add 14 oz meat/bones to recipe and add 4000 mg taurine)
7 oz chicken livers
2 cups water
4 egg yolks (raw egg whites contain avidin which depletes biotin in the body)
4000 mg wild salmon oil (never cod liver oil)
200 mg vitamin B complex
800 IU vitamin E
1.5 teaspoons lite iodized salt
4000 mg taurine additionally, if freezing for more than a week.

Directions:
1. Remove half of the skin and 20% of the bones from the chicken thighs and discard.
2. Rinse the meat, under cold running water, to remove surface bacteria.
3. Chunk up most of the muscle meat with poultry shears.
4. Grind the rest of the muscle meat, bones, skin, heart, and liver. Stir well.
5. Measure two cups of water into a bowl and whisk in the egg yolks, salmon oil, vitamin B complex, vitamin E, lite iodized salt, and added taurine (if using in place of hearts and/or adding because of freezing).
6. Mix the chunked meat, ground mixture, and supplement mixture together.
7. Fill containers. Leave room in the containers for expansion from freezing. Mark the containers with the contents and date and freeze.

Makes approximately 6¼ pounds (100 oz).
Cats eat about 4-5 ounces per day.
This recipe is not recommended for cats with chronic renal disease.

Appendix C

Rabbit & Chicken Combo
Ingredients:
3¾ pounds ground rabbit (ground rabbit typically includes the meat/bones/head which includes the heart, liver, and thyroid gland – check with your supplier)
¾ pound chicken thigh meat and skin (no bone)
14 oz chicken hearts (if not using – add 14 oz chicken meat/bones to recipe and add 4000 mg taurine)
0 or 7 oz chicken livers (if the ground rabbit contains liver – do not add)
2 cups water
4 egg yolks (raw egg whites contain avidin which depletes biotin in the body)
4000 mg wild salmon oil (never cod liver oil)
200 mg vitamin B complex
800 IU vitamin E
0 or 1.5 teaspoons lite iodized salt (if the ground rabbit contains the thyroid gland – do not add)
4000 mg taurine additionally, if freezing for more than a week

Directions:
1. Rinse the meat, under cold running water, to remove surface bacteria.
2. Chuck up most of the chicken muscle meat with poultry shears.
3. Grind the rest of the chicken muscle meat, skin, liver (if using), and heart (if using) and add to ground rabbit. Stir well.
4. Measure two cups of water into a bowl and whisk in the egg yolks, salmon oil, vitamin B complex, vitamin E, lite iodized salt (if using), and added taurine (if using in place of hearts and/or adding because of freezing).
5. Mix the chunked meat, ground mixture and supplement mixture together.
6. Fill containers. Leave room in the containers for expansion from freezing. Mark the containers with the contents and date and freeze.

Makes approximately 6¼ pounds (100 oz).
Cats eat about 4-5 ounces per day.
This recipe is not recommended for cats with chronic renal disease.

APPENDIX D

SUPPLIES FOR RAW CAT FOOD RECIPES

The following supplies are for the recipes listed in Appendix C. The brands listed are the ones I use; you may find other brands you'd prefer.

Tools:	Recommendations:
electric grinder	Tasin TS-108 meat grinder comes with the 4mm (5/32") grind plate needed. It will grind meat and bones. It is available at http://www.onestopjerkyshop.com
electronic scale	any digital scale that will weigh in pounds and ounces
poultry shears	purchase at local store or online
egg separator	if desired, you may use the shell halves instead
bowls	stainless steel is best or large container up to 40 pounds http://www.restockit.com/round-poly-container-22-quart-(11-0463).html
spoon or paddle	for stirring, paddle is used in large container batches http://www.restockit.com/36-stainless-steel-paddle-(13-0862).html
whisk	or a fork may be used
mortar & pestle	for grinding supplement tablets, unless capsules are used – stainless steel is best
freezer containers	plastic containers, glass containers, vacuum sealed bags, or zipper freezer bags
freezer space	space for the containers, may need additional freezer if you are making large batches

Appendix D

Ingredients:	Recommendations:
chicken thighs	free-range, antibiotic-free are best
rabbit	local market or east coast supplier http://hare-today.com/ or west coast supplier http://wholefoods4pets.com/
chicken heart	local butcher or above suppliers
chicken liver	local butcher or grocery store
chicken eggs	free-range, antibiotic-free are best
water	filtered tap water is best and cheapest way
taurine	powdered capsules – NOW® 1000mg
vitamin B complex	Country Life® Action B-100 tablets
vitamin E	dry capsules - TwinLab® E-400
wild salmon oil	capsules - (never cod liver oil) Carlson® Norwegian Salmon Oil
lite iodized salt	Morton's® Lite Salt™ Mixture contains potassium, sodium, iodine

The supplements listed above may be purchased from your local Whole Foods Market or ordered online from Amazon.com, iherb.com, Vitamin Shoppe or other distributor.

APPENDIX E
COST ANALYSIS

It goes without saying that a wet feline diet is more expensive than a dry one. Nevertheless, what you may spend for wet cat food per year could save you much more in future veterinary bills.

Taking into consideration digestibility, bioavailability, and caloric content, many of the more *expensive* high-meat-protein canned or raw foods when compared, are cheaper than the *cheap* brands when fed.

Cost Analysis of Commercially Prepared Wet Foods

Food	Fancy Feast® Elegant Medleys® White Meat Chicken Florentine (canned 3oz)	Wellness® Chicken Formula (canned 3oz)	Nature's Variety® Instinct® Raw Frozen Chicken (raw frozen medallion 1oz)
Kcal/oz	24	40	65
Price/oz (prices may vary in different markets)	$0.28	$0.40	$0.34
Cost/feeding 233 kcals per day*	$2.72	$2.33	$1.22
Bioavailability & Digestibility	acceptable	good	excellent

Based on daily caloric intake of a 12 pound adult cat.

On a daily caloric intake of 233 kilocalories, the most economical food represented here also has the best bioavailability and digestibility of the three: Nature's Variety® Instinct® Raw Chicken.

Appendix E

Cost Analysis of a Home-Prepared Raw Diet

The following analysis is based on figures for one batch of food in one market with meat ingredients purchased locally and supplements purchased through Amazon.com and its vendors (including shipping where applicable), using the Chicken Only recipe from Appendix C. All meat and organ products are from antibiotic-free chickens.

Ingredient	Price per Pound	Price per 4.5 Pound Recipe
Chicken Thigh with bone and skin	$1.79	$8.10
Chicken Liver	$1.49	$0.66
Chicken Heart	$1.49	$1.30

	Price Each	Price per 4.5 Pound Batch
Chicken Egg Yolk	$0.25	$1.00
Wild Salmon Oil	$0.32	$0.64
Vitamin B Complex	$0.32	$0.64
Vitamin E	$0.36	$0.72
Taurine	$0.18	$0.36
Lite Iodized Salt	*negligible*	*negligible*
TOTAL		**$13.42**
Total ounces of finished food (approx)		100
Price per ounce		$0.14
Cost per 5oz daily serving per cat		**$0.70**

Commercial pet food is taxed. None of the above ingredients are taxed.

ABOUT THE AUTHOR

Lynn, a former professionally-trained veterinary technician, has been a feline advocate for over two decades and has spent more than 25 years working in the fields of biology and chemistry. Lynn's experience with her own cats, one dying at nine years of age from chronic renal disease and the others diagnosed with varying medical ailments, inspired her to seek answers to their health challenges. Diet was the key.

Lynn's knowledge of feline nutrition lead to the creation of the *Feline Nutrition Awareness Effort,* an online venue founded to educate caregivers and advocate for optimum feline nutrition through a species-appropriate diet whether produced commercially or prepared at home.

INDEX

A

AAFCO. See Association of American Feed Control Officials
acid-base balance, 30, 31, 73
acidification, 39, 43
acidifiers, 43, 44, 66
acidifying diets, 45
acidosis, 43, 45
ad lib feeding, 73, 93
adult maintenance, 51, 52, 55, 63
adulteration, 50, 65
aflatoxin, 64
alcohol, 70
alkaline, 20, 31, 43, 73
allergen, 46
allergenic, 69
allergic, 64
alpha-amino acids. See amino acids
alpha-linolenic acid, 15, 16
amino acids, 2, 9, 10, 11, 13
amino sulfonic acid. See amino acids
ammonia, 12
ammonium, 29, 31, 43
ammonium chloride, 43, 66
amylase, 2, 19, 38
anabolism, 7
anchovy, 85
anemia, 31, 52
animal drugs, 49
animal fat, 67
anorexia, 41
antibiotics, 25, 26, 78
antimicrobial, 66
antioxidant, 25, 32, 41, 85
anti-vitamin, 66
arachidonic acid, 5, 16, 83
arginine, 11, 12
arsenic, 65
arthritis, 40
as fed, 54, 58, 62
ascorbic acid, 27
ash, 29, 69
Association of American Feed Control Officials, 49, 50
asthma, 48
avidin, 27, 79, 80, 84, 100, 101

B

B vitamins, 26, 85
bacteria, 7, 25, 26, 38, 64, 66, 69, 87, 89
balanced diets, 76, 91
barley, 64
beef, 69, 77, 78
beryllium, 65
beta-carotene, 3, 24, 84
BHA. See butylated hydroxyanisole
BHT. See butylated hydroxytoluene
bile salts, 2, 13
bioavailability, 9, 72, 90
biological contaminants, 64
biotin, 27, 79, 80, 84, 85, 100, 101
bisphenol A, 65, 87
black cats, 12
bleach solution, 89
blindness, 13
blood glucose. See diabetes
blood in the urine, 42
blood sugar. See diabetes
blood urea nitrogen, 45, 46, 72, 90
blood work, 75, 76
blue lips, 48
bone, 21, 25, 28, 29, 30, 31, 32, 43, 44, 77, 82
bone meal, 30
boron, 82
botulism, 64
bovine spongiform encephalitis, 78
BPA. See bisphenol A
BSE. See bovine spongiform encephalitis
building blocks, 10

BUN. *See* blood urea nitrogen
butylated hydroxyanisole, 64
butylated hydroxytoluene, 64
by-products, 68

C

cachexia, 47
cadmium, 65
calcium, 20, 25, 28, 29, 30, 32, 43, 44, 82
calcium apatite, 82
calcium oxalate stones, 27, 43, 66
calcium-phosphorus ratio, 33, 77
calcium-phosphorus-magnesium ratio, 32, 33, 96
caloric content, 53, 59, 62, 74
calories, 39, 53, 54, 59
Campylobacter, 89
cancer, 47, 48, 64
cancer cachexia, 47
canned food, 67, 70, 73, 76
carbohydrate metabolism, 43
carbohydrates, 18, 62, 67
carbon, 6
carcinogen, 67
cardiomyopathy, 13
carnassial teeth, 2
carnitine, 11, 13
carnivore, 1
carrageenan, 67
catabolism, 7
catalysts, 7
cation, 30
catnip, 21, 22
cecum, 4
cellulose, 20
Center for Veterinary Medicine, 49
cereal grains, 18
cheekbones, 2
chelated, 66
chemical contaminants, 64

chicken, 69, 77, 78
chicken gizzards, 70, 90
chicken hearts, 78, 79, 80, 83, 100, 101, 103
chicken livers, 79, 80, 83, 100, 101, 103
chloride, 31
choline, 27
chromosomes, 1
claws, 3
cobalamin, 26
cod liver oil, 85
co-enzyme Q10, 82, 83
collagen, 31, 83
commercial foods, 63, 81
complete and balanced, 50, 51, 56
constipation, 40, 42
contamination, 64
copper, 29, 31, 32, 66, 82, 84
corn, 18, 64, 67, 70
Cornish game hens, 78
cost analysis, 104, 105
coughing, 48
CRD. *See* renal disease
crystals, 29
culture and sensitivity, 43
CVM. *See* Center for Veterinary Medicine
cyanocobalamin, 26
cyanuric acid, 64
cysteine, 12, 13
cystitis, 42

D

D forms of amino acids, 11
daily caloric intake, 74, 96, 104
d-alpha-tocopherol. *See* vitamin E
deafness, 47
deficiencies, 91
dehydration, 5, 35, 43
dehydrocholesterol, 3, 25
dental health, 38, 78

Index

dentition, 1
depth perception, 3
desert, 5, 31, 34, 43, 45, 69
DHA. *See* docosahexaenoic acid
diabetes, 5, 19, 26, 37, 40, 41, 42, 67, 72, 75, 91, 92
diarrhea, 26, 46, 68, 72, 90, 94
diet change, 42, 75, 76, 90, 92, 93
digestibility, 8, 71, 90
digestion, 7
digestive transit time, 3, 89
dilated cardiomyopathy, 13
disease, 37
disinfecting, 89
DL-methionine, 43, 44, 66
DNA, 1
docosahexaenoic acid, 15, 16, 17, 65, 85, 86
drinking, 26
dry coat, 40, 47
dry food, 64, 69, 73, 89
dry matter, 35, 58, 59, 61, 62, 69, 97
dry skin, 72, 90

E

E. coli, 91
ear, 47
ear infections, 47
EFAs. *See* omega-EFAs
egg whites, 27, 45, 46, 47, 79, 80, 84, 100, 101
egg yolks, 79, 80, 84
eicosapentaenoic acid, 15, 16, 17, 47, 65, 85, 86
elderly people, 89
electrolytes, 31
energy, 7, 10, 15
enzymes, 7, 9, 10
EPA. *See* eicosapentaenoic acid
essential amino acids. *See* amino acids
essential fatty acids. *See* omega-EFAs

ethoxyquin, 64
eyes, 2

F

facultative, 1
fat, 12, 15, 25, 83
fatty acid synthesis, 26
fatty liver disease. *See* hepatic lipidosis
FCV. *See* feline calicivirus
FDA. *See* Food and Drug Administration
Federal Food, Drug and Cosmetic Act, 49
Federal Trade Commission, 49
feed ingredients, 49
feed laws, 49
feeding raw food, 88
feeding schedule, 73, 93
feeding trial, 50
feeding tube, 41
feedings, 73, 74
feline calicivirus, 38
feline herpes virus, 12
feline immunodeficiency virus, 38
feline lower urinary tract disorder, 42
feline oral resorptive lesions, 39
feline spongiform encephalitis, 78
felinine, 12
fiber, 20
fish, 41, 64, 69, 77, 84
fish body oil, 47, 67, 85
FIV. *See* feline immunodeficiency virus
flaxseed oil, 15, 47, 67
flora. *See* gut flora
flu, 12
fluoride, 82
FLUTD. *See* feline lower urinary tract disorder
food additives, 49
food allergy, 69
Food and Drug Administration, 49, 56
food poisoning, 89

Food Safety Modernization Act, 50
FORLs. *See* feline oral resorptive lesions
free-choice feeding. *See* ad lib feeding
freezer bags, 86
freezing, 79, 81
fructokinase, 19
fructose, 19
fruit, 18, 68
FSE. *See* feline spongiform encephalitis
FSMA. *See* Food Safety Modernization Act
FTC. *See* Federal Trade Commission
fungi, 64, 89
FUS, 30, 42

G

gagging, 48
garlic, 67
gastrointestinal, 30
gastrointestinal problems, 46, 68
gastrointestinal tract, 89, 93
Generally Recognized as Safe, 52
generator, 87
genetically modified organisms, 67
gingivitis, 38, 39
glucokinase, 19
glucose, 12, 18, 19, 27, 39
glucose conversion, 19
glycemic index, 42
glycine, 12
GMOs. *See* genetically modified organisms
gourmet pet food, 54
grain-free, 67, 69, 71
grains, 18, 64, 67
GRAS. *See* Generally Recognized as Safe
grasses, 18, 21
grind, 79
grinder, 77, 78, 79, 102
grinding, 79, 81
growth and reproduction, 51, 52

growth hormones, 78
guaranteed analysis, 54, 58
gum disease, 38
gut flora, 7, 25, 26, 66

H

hairballs, 72, 90
halitosis, 38
hearing, 3, 47
heart disease, 47, 48
heartworm infection, 48
heavy metal contamination, 65, 77
Heinz body anemia, 66, 67
Heinz body formations, 52
hemoglobin, 31, 66, 84
hepatic enzymes, 19, 39, 45
hepatic lipidosis, 12, 14, 19, 40, 41, 75
herpes virus, 12
hexokinase, 2, 19
high blood pressure. *See* hypertension
high-fiber diets, 40, 42, 44
histidine, 11
Hodgkins, Elizabeth, DVM, 95
homemade diet, 76, 81
hormones, 10
houseplants, 21
hunger switch, 40
hydration, 69
hydrogen peroxide, 89
hydroxylapatite, 82
hyperallergenic, 77
hyperammonemia, 12
hypercalcemia. *See* idiopathic hypercalcemia
hyperglycemia. *See* diabetes
hypertension, 30, 46
hyperthyroidism, 46, 67
hypoallergenic diets, 46, 47
hypoglycemia, 39, 42, 72, 91, 92
hypoglycemic shock, 75

I

IBD. See irritable bowel disease
idiopathic, 37
idiopathic hypercalcemia, 43, 44, 45, 66
immune system compromised, 89
immunostimulator, 32
indoor cats, 37, 63
inflammatory process, 32
inflammatory response, 16
inorganic, 28
inorganic salts, 66
insoluble fiber, 20
insulin, 18, 39, 41, 42
intestinal flora. See gut flora
intestinal length, 4
intestine, 3, 4, 66, 89
iodine, 32, 86
ionized calcium, 44
iron, 27, 29, 31, 66
irradiation, 65
irritable bowel disease, 5, 35, 46, 67, 72, 91
isoleucine, 11
itchy skin, 47

J

Jacobson's organ, 22
jaws, 2

K

kidney disease. See renal disease
kidney stones, 30
kidneys, 43, 44, 45
kilocalories, 54
kitten food, 63

L

L forms of amino acids, 11
labels, 49, 50, 54, 58
lactose intolerant, 68
lamb, 69
leucine, 11
life stages, 51, 52
lignins, 20
linoleic acid, 5, 16, 83
liver, 12, 41, 75
liver enzymes, 10, 19
longevity, 37, 94
low blood glucose. See hypoglycemia
low-calorie cat food, 52
lungworms, 48
lysine, 11, 12, 82
lysozyme, 38, 89

M

macrominerals, 28
mad cow disease, 78
magnesium, 29, 30, 31, 32, 43, 44, 82
magnesium restriction, 39
manganese, 32, 82
ME Profile. See metabolizable energy profile
meal, chicken, 68
meat, 68, 81
meat meal, 67
medicated feeds, 49
melamine, 64
melanin, 12
menadione, 66
menaquinone, 66
mercury, 65, 77
metabolic pathways, 5, 6, 7, 8, 9
metabolism, 6, 7
metabolizable energy profile, 58, 59, 60
metalloproteinases, 32
methionine, 11, 12, 13
methylcobalamin, 26, 46
microminerals, 28
microorganisms, 7
microwaving, 88

Feline Nutrition

milk, 68
minerals, 28
minimums and maximums, 55, 58
mites, storage, 64
moisture content, 54
molars, 2
mold, 64, 69, 89
mouth, 39, 89

N

National Research Council, 49
natural pet food, 54
neck lesions. *See* feline oral resorptive lesions
nepetalactone, 21
niacin, 26, 84
nitrogen, 6, 10, 12
non-essential amino acids, 11
NRC. *See* National Research Council
nutrient percentages, 60, 97
nutrient profiles, 50, 51, 55, 86
nutrition, 6
nutritional adequacy statement, 51

O

oats, 64
obese, 40, 42, 74, 75, 93
obesity, 5, 19, 39, 40, 67
obligate carnivores, 1, 9, 11
omega-3 EFAs, 16, 47, 81, 85
omega-6 EFAs, 16, 47
omega-EFAs, 15, 16, 67, 79, 85, 87
onions, 67
organic pet food, 7, 10, 21, 55, 56, 69, 70, 78
ornithine, 12
oropharynx, 38
otitis, 47
overnutrition, 56
overweight, 40, 74, 75, 90, 93
oxalate, 27

oxidation, 25, 64, 79, 85

P

pancreas, 18, 39, 41
pancreatitis, 41
papillae, 2
parasites, 87
peas, 67
percent body weight, 75, 96
percentage calculations, 96
percentage of calories, 58, 60, 98
percentage of dry matter weight, 60, 98
percentage of food weight, 60, 97
pet food, 49, 50, 51
pet food cans, 65
pet food complaint, 56
phenylalanine, 11
phosphate, 29, 31
phosphate binders, 45, 46
phosphoric acid, 66
phosphorus, 25, 29, 32, 43, 45, 82
phylloquinone, 66
phytate, 29
Pierson, Lisa, DVM, 76, 95
play session, 93
polymers, 10
polyunsaturated fats, 41
pork, 78
potassium, 30, 31, 82
potatoes, 67
poultry shears, 78
premium pet food, 54
preservatives, 64
processing, 66
product names, 53
propylene glycol, 52
protein, 10, 45, 69
protein metabolism, 10, 45, 46, 72, 90
proteinated, 66
psyllium husk, 20

Q

quail, 78

R

rabbit, 69, 71, 78, 80, 81, 101, 103
racemic, 11
rat carcass, 55, 86
raw food, 70, 73, 76, 91, 100, 102
recalls, 64
regurgitation, 94
renal disease, 4, 5, 26, 35, 44, 45, 46, 69, 76, 80, 81, 93, 95
rendering, 68
retinol, 24
retinyl palmitate, 25
rice, 64

S

safety of raw food, 89
Safety Reporting Portal, 56, 95
sagittal crest, 2
saliva, 2, 19, 38, 89
salmon, 85
salmon oil, 47, 67, 79, 80, 81, 85, 100, 101, 103
Salmonella, 64, 89
salt, 47, 79, 80, 81, 86, 100, 101, 103
sardine, 85
scale, 75, 95, 102
scent marking, 12
seafood, 26
seaweed, 67
selenium, 32, 65, 82, 83
self-limit, 40
semi-moist foods, 52, 70
senior cat foods, 52
shortness of breath, 48
silica, 82
skin, 47, 64
skin, chicken, 83

skull, 2
snacks. *See* treats
sodium, 31, 82
sodium bisulfate, 66
sodium selenate, 65
sodium selenite, 65
soy products, 46, 64, 67
starches, 19, 70
stomach, 4, 20
stomatitis, 38, 39
stones, 29
stool odor, 72, 90
storing raw food, 86, 87
struvite crystals, 29, 30, 31, 43
subcutaneous fluid therapy, 46
sucrose, 19
sugar, blood. *See* diabetes
sugar, taste. *See* sweet detectors
super premium pet food, 54
supplements, 66
surface bacteria, 77
sweet detectors, 4, 19, 20, 70
synthetic versions, 66

T

tartar control, 38
taste. *See* sweet detectors
taurine, 2, 11, 12, 13, 20, 78, 79, 80, 81, 83, 85, 100, 103
taurine deficiency, 13
teeth, 1, 25, 28, 29, 38, 39, 82
thawing raw food, 87, 88
therapeutic foods, 70
thiamin, 26, 64, 77, 84
thiamin deficiency, 84
thiaminase, 26, 77, 84
thiosulfate compounds, 67
thirst, 45
thirst drive, 35, 43
threonine, 11, 12
thyroid gland, 32, 86

Feline Nutrition

thyroid hormone, 46, 86
thyroxine, 32
tocopherol. *See* vitamin E
tongue, 2, 19
tooth decay, 38
tooth resorption. *See* feline oral resorptive lesions
toxicities, 91
treats, 44, 70, 73, 90
trichinosis, 78
triglycerides, 15, 18
tryptophan, 11, 26
tumor growth, 47
tuna, 65, 77, 93
turkey, 69, 78
tyrosine, 12

U

ubiquinone. *See* co-enzyme Q10
ultra premium pet food, 54
underweight, 90
United States Department of Agriculture, 49
upper respiratory infection, 48
urea, 29, 83
urethra, 43
urethral blockage. *See* urinary tract blockage
urinary bladder, 42, 43
urinary diets, 43, 44, 66
urinary health, 69
urinary tract blockage, 29, 43
urinary tract infection, 42
urinary tract problems, 5, 35, 39, 42, 43, 72, 77, 91
urination, 26, 45
urine, 27, 31, 35, 43, 44, 72, 90
urine pH, 30, 43, 44
uroliths, 29, 42
USDA. *See* United States Department of Agriculture

V

vaccine protocols, 38
valine, 11
vegetable oils, 67
vegetables, 18, 20, 68
veterinarian, 75, 76, 91, 92
vibrissae, 3
vinegar, 89
vision, 2
vitamin A, 3, 24, 25, 65, 84
vitamin B complex, 46, 79, 80, 81, 85, 100, 101, 103
vitamin B1, 26, 77
vitamin B12, 26, 46
vitamin B3, 26
vitamin B7, 27
vitamin C, 27
vitamin D, 3, 25, 82
vitamin E, 25, 32, 41, 64, 79, 80, 82, 85, 87, 100, 101, 103
vitamin K, 25, 81, 83, 84
vitamin K1, 66
vitamin K2, 66
vitamin K3, 66
vitamins, 24
vomeronasal organ, 22
vomiting, 46, 72, 90
vomitoxin, 64

W

warming raw food, 88
water, 4, 34, 35, 36, 43, 45, 69, 84
water, ingested, 34
water, metabolic, 34
weight gain, 52, 74
weight loss, 40, 41, 74, 75, 93
weight management food, 40
wheat, 64, 70
wheezing, 48
whiskers, 3

Wille, Natascha, 76

Y

yeast, 7, 68
young children, 89

Z

zinc, 29, 32, 64, 82
zygomatic arches, 2

REFERENCES

[1] Heffner RS, Heffner HE. Hearing range of the domestic cat. Hear Res. 1985;19(1):85-8. PubMed PMID:4066516.

[2] Heffner.

[3] Hand, MS, CD Thatcher, RL Remillard, P Roudebush. *Small Animal Clinical Nutrition*, 4th Edition. Mark Morris Institute. Marceline, MO: Walsworth Publishing Company, 2000. 297.

[4] Hand 297.

[5] Morris, JG, Rogers QR. *Comparative aspects of nutrition and metabolism of dogs and cats*. In: Burger IH, Rivers JPW, eds. Nutrition of the Dog and Cat. Cambridge, UK: Cambridge University Press, 1989. 35-66.

[6] Hand 297.

[7] Li X, Li W, Wang H, Cao J, Maehashi K, et al. (2005) Pseudogenization of a Sweet-Receptor Gene Accounts for Cats' Indifference Toward Sugar. PLoS Genet 1(1): e3. doi:10.1371/journal.pgen.0010003.

[8] "Nutrition." Merriam-Webster Dictionary Online. 2010. Encyclopedia Britannica Company. 16 January 2011 http://www.merriam-webster.com/.

[9] Pion PD, Kittleson MD, Skiles ML, Rogers QR, Morris JG. Dilated cardiomyopathy associated with taurine deficiency in the domestic cat: relationship to diet and myocardial taurine content. Adv Exp Med Biol. 1992;315:63-73. PubMed PMID: 1387282.

[10] Subcommittee on Cat Nutrition, Committee on Animal Nutrition, Board on Agriculture, National Research Council. *Nutrient Requirements in Cats*. Revised Edition. Washington, D.C.: National Academy Press, 1986. 7.

[11] Li X.

[12] Li X.

[13] American Chemical Society. "Catnip Repels Mosquitoes More Effectively Than DEET." ScienceDaily, 28 Aug. 2001. Web. 15 Jun. 2011.

[14] Siegal, Mordecai, Ed. *The Cornell Book of Cats*, 2nd. Edition. Cornell Feline Health Center, Cornell University. Villard, 1987. 82.

References

[15] Siegal 82.

[16] Siegal 82.

[17] Siegal 82.

[18] Kutsky, RJ. Phosphorous. In: Handbook of Vitamins, Minerals and Hormones. Van Nostrand Reinhold Company, NewYork, 1981. 4.

[19] Wille, Natascha. Raw Meat Cat Food Website. 2010. http://rawmeatcatfood.com. Path: Cat Nutrition; Magnesium.

[20] Wille, Magnesium.

[21] Wille, Magnesium.

[22] Wille, Magnesium.

[23] Skoch, ER, Chandler, EA, Douglas, GM and Richardson, DP (1991), Influence of diet on urine pH and the Feline urological syndrome. Journal of Small Animal Practice, 32: 413–419. doi: 10.1111/j.1748-5827.1991.tb00968.x

[24] Wille, Magnesium.

[25] Wille, Magnesium.

[26] Anderson, RS. Water balance in the dog and cat. *J Small Animal Practice*, 1982;23:588-598.

[27] Forrester, S Dru. *Management of Feline Lower Urinary Tract Disease*. Hills Symposium on Urinary Tract Disease. Hill's Pet Nutrition Inc. Topeka, KS. 2007. 46.

[28] Funaba M, Yamate T, Hashida Y, Maki K, Gotoh K, Kaneko M, Yamamoto H, Iriki T, Hatano Y, Abe M. Effects of a high-protein diet versus dietary supplementation with ammonium chloride on struvite crystal formation in urine of clinically normal cats. Am J Vet Res. 2003 Aug;64(8):1059-64. PubMed PMID: 12926602.

[29] Chew, Dennis. *Hypercalcemia in Cats*. World Small Animal Veterinary Association. Vancouver, Canada. 2001.

[30] Midkiff, A., Chew, D., Randolph, J., Center, S. and DiBartola, S. (2000), Idiopathic Hypercalcemia in Cats. Journal of Veterinary Internal Medicine, 14: 619–626. doi: 10.1111/j.1939-1676.2000.tb02286.x

[31] Markwell, Peter. *Recent Advances in the Dietary Management of Chronic Renal Failure in Cats*. World Small Animal Veterinary Association. Vancouver, Canada. 2001.

[32] Ogilvie, Gregory K. *Nutrition and Cancer: Exciting Advances for 2002*. World Small Animal Veterinary Association. Granada, Spain. 2002.

[33] Ogilvie.

[34] Vondruska, JF. The effect of a rat carcass diet on the urinary pH of the cat. Comparison Animal Practice. 1987;1 (August): 5-9.

[35] Association of American Feed Control Officials. Official Publication. 1998.

[36] National Toxicology Program. *Tox-38-Sodium Selenate and Sodium Selenite (CAS Nos. 13410-01-0 and 10102-18-8)*. US Department of Health and Human Services. 1994.

[37] RSPCA Australia. What is RSPCA Australia's position on the irradiation of imported pet food products? http://kb.rspca.org.au/What-is-RSPCA-Australias-position-on-the-irradiation-of-imported-pet-food-products_307.html. 2011

[38] RSPCA Australia.

[39] Atkins, P, Ernyei, L, Driscoll, W, et. al. *Analysis of Toxic Trace Metals in Pet Foods Using Cryogenic Grinding and Quantitation by ICP-MS, Part II*. Spectroscopy Magazine. (February 2011). 42-59.

[40] Wille, Natascha. Raw Meat Cat Food Website. 1997. http://rawmeatcatfood.com. Path: Recipes; Orginal Raw Meat Cat Food Recipe.

[41] "Nutrition Facts". Self Nutrition Data. Condé Nast Digital. 24 January 2011 http://nutritiondata.self.com. Keyword: raw chicken thigh skin.

[42] "Nutrition Facts". Self Nutrition Data. Condé Nast Digital. 24 January 2011 http://nutritiondata.self.com. Keyword: raw chicken fryer skin only.

[43] "Nutrition Facts". Self Nutrition Data. Condé Nast Digital. 24 January 2011 http://nutritiondata.self.com. Keyword: raw chicken heart.

[44] "Nutrition Facts". Self Nutrition Data. Condé Nast Digital. 24 January 2011 http://nutritiondata.self.com. Keyword: raw chicken liver.

[45] "Nutrition Facts". Self Nutrition Data. Condé Nast Digital. 24 January 2011 http://nutritiondata.self.com. Keyword: raw egg yolk fresh.

References

[46] Vondruska 5-9.

[47] Malik, Richard. *Controversies in Feline Nutrition.* World Small Animal Veterinary Association. Prague, Czech Republic. 2006.

Printed in Great Britain
by Amazon